CONFLICT IN CULTURE

Permissions Versus
Controls and
Alcohol Use in
American Society

John E. Tropman

The University of Michigan

UNIVERSITY
PRESS OF
AMERICA

LANHAM • NEW YORK • LONDON

Copyright © 1986 by

University Press of America,® Inc.

4720 Boston Way
Lanham, MD 20706

3 Henrietta Street
London WC2E 8LU England

All rights reserved

Printed in the United States of America

Library of Congress Cataloging in Publication Data

Tropman, John E.
 Conflict in culture.

 Bibliography: p.
 Includes indexes.
 1. Drinking of alcoholic beverages—United States—
History. 2. Drinking of alcoholic beverages—Moral and
ethical aspects. 3. Social norms. I. Title.
HV5292.T76 1986   394.1'3'0973   85-31511
ISBN 0-8191-5246-3 (alk. paper)
ISBN 0-8191-5247-1 (pbk. : alk. paper)

All University Press of America books are produced on acid-free
paper which exceeds the minimum standards set by the National
Historical Publications and Records Commission.

This volume is dedicated to my children,
Sarah, Jessica, and Matthew Tropman,
in the hope of aiding them in understanding
the balances between permissions and controls.

ACKNOWLEDGEMENTS

Many people assisted with this manuscript. Edith Gomberg initially interested me in the area of alcohol. Craig King and Kim Hoa Granville helped in the early phases and Sharon Jablonski assisted in later phases. Bill Birdsall read and commented on many parts. Stannette Amy provided invaluable intellectual help and checked the entire manuscript. Dean Harold R. Johnson of the School of Social Work provided financial assistance which helped this project to completion, but more importantly provided intellectual stimulation and support. To all these and others who were involved in various phases of this project, my deep appreciation.

A special thanks goes to Daniel Madaj. While he took responsibility for manuscript preparation his contribution extended far beyond that. His scholarly influence can be felt throughout the book.

I would like to thank the Journal of Sociology and Social Welfare for permission to use portions of the text, Figure 2 and Figure 5 in this book, which appeared in "A Contest of Values" (Vol. IX, No. 2, June 1982).

CONFLICT IN CULTURE: PERMISSIONS VERSUS CONTROLS AND ALCOHOL USE IN AMERICAN SOCIETY

Table of Contents

Preface		ix
Introduction		xi
Chapter 1:	Conflict in Culture	1
	The Social and Cultural System
The Structure of Culture
Change in Culture and Structure
Conclusion	
Chapter 2:	Permission and Control	9
	Social and Cultural Order
Permission and Control
A Cyclical Approach
Conclusion	
Chapter 3:	Alcohol and American Society	15
	Control in American History
Ambivalence and Alcohol
Alcohol as Metaphor
Conclusion	
Chapter 4:	Historical Periods in the Permission/Control Balance	25
	The Repentant Drinker
The Enemy Drinker
The Sick Drinker
The Responsible Drinker
Conclusion	
Chapter 5:	Loci of Permission/Control	43
	Crucial Variables in the Locus of Permission/Control	

              Voluntary Versus Government
              Collegial Versus Familial
              Drinking Versus Alcoholism
              Rationality Versus Non-rationality
              (or Fault Versus No-Fault)
              Internal Versus External Control
              Mastery Versus Drift
              Conclusion

Chapter 6:	Permission and Control in a Communal Society	77

              The Communal Society
              Conclusion

References	87
Bibliography	92
Author Index	99
Subject Index	101
About the Author	104

PREFACE

For some time I have been working on the idea that we learn values in pairs of partially contradictory concepts - like achievement and equality (Lipset, 1963), adequacy and equity (Cohen, 1977), among others. This volume is one attempt to put that concept into operation within an analytical frame of reference. It has been discussed elsewhere (Tropman, 1978) and a major summary of this perspective is in preparation in a volume called <u>American Values and Social Welfare</u> (forthcoming). A second volume, <u>Kaleidoscope of Culture</u> (forthcoming) seeks to put this perspective to use in looking at changes in public opinion over time. Taken together, these works provide at least a convincing argument that a dualistic approach to thinking about values is useful and illuminating. This volume does not seek to add to the literature on the history of alcohol attitudes [Rorabaugh (1979) has done a more comprehensive job of that]; rather, it seeks to interpret that history, and thus look at it in a fresh perspective, and perhaps contribute to the literature on values as well. I would like to stress that it is a preliminary and exploratory effort, one which is aimed at stimulating thinking rather than stopping it; at posing questions rather than answering them, at introducing new perspectives rather than refining old ones. It is an initial step on a longer journey of exploration in the field of cultural conflict. I hope therefore that readers will view it in this spirit - as a beginning point for discussion, as a stimulus for comment and research. If one can come away from it with the thought, "Now that it is an interesting idea - I'll have to think more about it," my goal will have been achieved.

INTRODUCTION

This volume has several purposes, with each having equal importance if not equal treatment.

First, it is an occasion to explore a particular perspective on the structure of culture - a dualistic perspective - which I believe is an important alternative to a view which looks at values on a one by one basis.

Second, one particular value conflict - that between the social supply of permission (freedom, liberty, independence) and the supply of control (internal or external, voluntary or coercive) - is explored in some detail, and with reference to changes in the social approach to alcohol use in American history.

Third, it outlines, in a general way, the historical shifts of attitudes toward alcohol over the history of the United States.

Fourth, it conceptualizes certain themes and variations in the country's treatment of alcohol over the years. If, as I suspect, the historical picture is best described by a cyclical rather than a linear pattern then perhaps we can anticipate what some of the future crises and difficulties might be.*

Finally, it illuminates some basic social and cultural processes that operate in American society. Alcohol attitudes and approaches are not segregated "off" in some attitudinal wasteland, but are related to, and sometimes manifestations of, central features of the American value and cultural structure. This link gives alcohol study a wider relevance.

* It may be a spiral pattern. See Tropman and Erlich (1974).

CHAPTER ONE

CONFLICT IN CULTURE

All studies proceed from a frame of reference or a point of view. This effort is no exception. Because the perspective used here differs a bit from the usual "values analysis," a brief detour must be taken to explain it. But it is a detour only with respect to the attention to alcohol issues, and sets the stage for considering them in detail. This will permit a richer and fuller understanding of the major portion of this volume, which is an application to the field of alcohol attitudes and behaviors.

The Social and Cultural System

The study of society can be divided into two main parts; the social system (which focuses upon what people actually do, the behaviors they exhibit, the laws which are passed, and so on), and the actual artifacts of society (and the cultural system or the set of beliefs, values attitudes which characterize a particular society). As Anderson suggested, "social order refers to ascertainable patterns of regular structure, process, or change occurring in or resulting from human interaction" (Anderson, 1964, p. 660). It contains elements of both disorganization and "approved" organization.

The term cultural order refers to the cultural system in the same way that social order refers to the social system. Sometimes it's called "the moral order" or phrases like norms or mores are used.

> [Moral order] . . . or normative order is a term used to denote (a) the system of values (q.v.) and

norms which govern social behaviour in a group or society and/or (b) the behaviour so governed or the order discoverable in the behaviour so governed, insofar as that behaviour or order conforms to and is to some degree the product of the system of norms and values (Kolb, 1964, p. 443).

Social order and moral order are ways of talking about the known patterns or structures in our interaction with people and with pattern and structure in our thoughts, norms, values, etc.

Naturally, these two major subsystems interact. A Marxian perspective suggests that the social system is the independent one exercising dominant power and force, and that the system of values and beliefs is subordinate, changing in response to developments in the social structure. Alternately, a perspective developed by Max Weber (1956) suggests that values are the dominant force and that adjustments in the social structure follow from changes in values. This argument is the old "pen versus sword" argument, and will not be resolved here. Rather, my perspective is that each system is important, and each generates changes in the other.

This process of mutual adjustment may occur relatively immediately, or may take place over time, with one system "lagging" behind the other. Ogburn (1968) named a situation in which changes in social structure were ahead of adaptations in the cultural system as "cultural lag." One could also think of "social lag" as occuring when changes in the patterns of behavior adapt more slowly than patterns of values. The fulcrum of this volume, therefore, is the exploration of the social and cultual structure and their interrelationships, with special reference to alcohol attitudes and related activities.

The Structure of Culture

Much work in sociology has been done on the structure of the social system but less is available which details the values/normative system of the society. Most of the work on values (Williams, 1968, 1969, 1970; Rokeach, 1979) assumes that values come in "strings" or "lists." Often, social commentators assume that a society is characterized by a particular value - commitment to independence, for example - and then examples of compliance with or divergence from this value are explored. And these lists do, indeed, form a sort of dictionary of culture, giving the important words and commitments which are important to a particular society. But just as an analysis of language requires not only the parts but also the rules through which the parts are combined, so the study of culture requires a grammar, or set of rules through which the parts are structured, positioned, combined. I make no claim to offer a complete set of rules; only one seems sufficiently reasonable to be suggested here. It is a proposition which argues that values come in juxtaposed sets, and that we learn them in that way, so that focus upon one automatically generates a consideration of the other.

This conception of "values pairs" has emerged at various points in the sociological literature more as an analytic device than a proposition or hypothesis. Lynd (1939) used a set of such juxtaposed values to look at American society, as did Lipset in his book, The First New Nation. Lipset used only one master conflict, however - one between commitments to achievement and to equality - as his central organizing concept, while Lynd gave many examples of cultural conflicts. Yinger uses a similar concept in his conception of countercultures (1982). Edelman looks at political life through a dual-values approach (1977) and Cumming, in an analysis similar to this one, looks at the allocation of resources to the mentally ill through such a lens (1967). I have used this perspective to consider attitudes toward welfare (1978) and changes in public opinion over time (Tropman, forthcoming). This analysis is a continuation of the effort to use a dual-values perspective to illuminate our understanding of society in general, and

American society in particular.

At this stage of development, the idea that values come in linked pairs, each somewhat at variance with the other, should be regarded as an hypothesis, to be tested in a series of investigations. And indeed, the utility of such a perspective as used here and elsewhere is one kind of test. Edelman, in his study of political myths, puts it well:

> We find, then, a pair of opposing political myths for each of the conflicting cognitive patterns that define our attitudes toward social problems, the authorities who deal with them, the people who suffer from them. Ambivalence is reflected in concomitant myths, each of them internally consistent, though they are inconsistent with each other. At the same time the availability in the culture of opposing belief permits the individual to reconcile contradictions and live with his or her ambivalence (Edelman, 1977, p. 8).

He adds:

> Both patterns of belief are present in our culture and our minds (Edelman, 1977, p. 7).

Erickson finds this value conflict perspective useful in looking at the culture and structure of Appalachia.

> Any list of "traits" seems to have a certain consistency when the items are laid out one after the other in a written account, but human experience is not arranged in so linear a form. The items themselves are part of a continuous whole, an entire

> package; and when one looks back over the list of traits . . . it becomes hard to avoid the conclusion that there is a good deal of contradiction and discrepancy there (Erikson, 1972, p. 77).

He goes on to point out that the people of Appalachia are warm but suspicious; independent, yet dependent; fierce, yet passive; and so on. And it is this perception of dual commitments, each challenging the other, which makes the analysis so useful.

For purposes of this exploration of the history of alcohol in American society, only one pair of conflicting values is used - values of permission and values of control. Naturally, this value pair is not the only one which impacts on alcohol attitudes, but it is certainly among the more important. Too, this value pair has applications which go well beyond alcohol, and some of these links will be mentioned. A more detailed discussion of permission and control is presented in Chapter Two. Suffice it to note here that in such an exploratory effort as this one, limit and focus improves the acuteness of the analysis.

Change in Culture and Structure

The history of alcohol in American society is a history of change. As such, it is a history of values change. One might ask how, and why, values change. The ability to deal with values change is one of the more important aspects of a value conflict perspective. First, of course, is the matter of values tension, or what Erikson called "contradiction and discrepancy." If one assumes that values exist in conflicting pairs, then conflict between pair members and among sets is the norm, not the exception. And the tension which characterizies this conflict can be a source of energy for change. As Lipset suggests (1963), emphasis upon achievement in American history led to conflict with norms of equality; these norms in turn demanded attention, which generated conflict with achievement orientation, etc. With respect to the present study, emphasis upon social control conflicts with commitments to freedom; too much freedom demands more control. Hence, the linked nature of conflicting commitments creates an engine of change.

But there is another mechanism as well. Hirshman (1982) talks about disappointment as an important generator of change. Any given value emphasis is likely, over time, to become disappointing. This leads to a search for an alternative place to locate one's attention. In Hirshman's analysis, swings from public orientation to private emphases, back to public orientation and so on occupy his discussion. But the mechanism he suggests is entirely general. Hence, it is not only the conflict created by attending to one value and ignoring another that may stimulate change; it is also the disappointment with the value posture one is emphasizing that is important. Hence, there is a pull (tension) and a push (disappointment) in the system which work together to produce cultural change.

Pressures internal to the cultural system, however, are not the only source of change in that system. Pressures from the social system (as Marx might have put it) are important, too. Changes in the availability of alcohol, or its price, may, in the shorter or longer run, cause changes in attitudes toward it; it works the other way too - changes in the cultural system might cause more or less alcohol to be available. In other words, changes in one of the major subsystems may cause greater supply of permissions or controls; these in turn interact with the initiating system.

One further point is worth stressing here. The conflicting-values approach means that there can be change and stability within the system at the same time. Emphasis upon a particular value pair can shift, with one being more dominant than another at a particular point in time. But these are emphases, not complete rejection of one and acceptance of another (although there surely are individuals within any population who might be characterized in this way). Often, such change is characterized as a "return" to "traditional" values (whether, as in Lipset's case, these values are ones of achievement or values of equality)! Traditional, within the value conflict perspective, means "the values we were not emphasizing at the moment, but to which we still have strong commitments." This pattern may emerge as a cyclical alternation between pairs of values something which certainly characterizes American alcohol history.

In short, each subsystem has mechanisms of change which are contained within itself and each system is affected by developments in the other. The speed of cultural/structural articulation, as mentioned a moment ago, is a factor as well. "Lags" can occur either in the cultural structure (cultural lag) in adjusting to the social structure, or in the social structure (social lag) in adjusting to the cultural system. The key element here is time, and change over time. That is why an historical perspective, which is the focus of Chapter Four, is so important. History, from this change-oriented perspective, is the process of cultural and social adjustment. Each adjustment represents a moment-in-time solution to a number of time-specific social and cultural forces, which themselves keep changing, rendering the moment-in-time solution out of date in short order. It is from this perspective that changes in alcohol posture are interpreted.

But perhaps analysis over time misses a focus on important components within time. Chapter Five emphasizes a different aspect of the permission/control conflict - a range of loci where permission/control conflicts occur. In a situation of dynamic balance, like a society, changes over time are the result of rebalancing of multiple structures at any moment in time. Hence, both "longitudinal" and "cross sectional" perspectives are necessary.

Conclusion

Society is composed of a social system and a cultural system, a set of specific actions, behaviors, laws, artifacts, and a set of beliefs, values, and attitudes. There a continual tension between these two systems, and each can change and cause, in turn, changes in the other system. When the social system changes more slowly than the cultural system, a condition of "social lag" exists; when the reverse obtains, it is called cultural lag. In the case of alcohol, attention to both social features (kind, amount, supply, etc.) and cultural features (norms about when to drink, who can drink, how one drinks, etc.) are each important. In the main, this study focuses upon the cultural system and its relationship to alcohol use.

Most of the attention to the cultural system has been in the form of a "dictionary" of values, or lists of commitments which people have and to which they profess commitment. Less attention has been paid to the structure of the value system, the way in which values fit together, or what might be called a "grammar of values." In this volume an hypothesis about this grammar is advanced, viz., that values come in pairs or sets of two, each somewhat opposed to the other, such as the values of achievement and the values of equality. In this case, the values of particular interest are those of permission to drink, and of control of drinking. Supplies of permissions and supplies of controls are both needed, and are always in conflict with each other, to some degree. Emphasis on one leads to a deemphasis upon the other, causing values tension and pressure for rebalance. In addition, disappointment in the attention to one value sets up a separate, but related, pressure for change. Hence, cultural change can be seen, from this perspective at least, as a process of alternation between conflicting, but linked, values. Such a process certainly describes the history of alcohol in the United States. In the remainder of this volume the details of this assertion will be explored.

CHAPTER TWO

PERMISSION AND CONTROL

Social and Cultural Order

Unquestionably, social and personal order are among the most important elements in a society's development of social and cultural structure. It is the way these structures characterize the society as a whole, the individuals within society, and the ways individuals/society interact that, over time, come to be identified as the "patterns of culture" (Benedict, 1946) which we attribute to society and nation. Any sociological history must identify the historical patterns and shifts over time. But such order, at either level, does not come automatically. In some sense, society "controls" us with an eye toward securing agreement with (or at least conformity to) the extant social and cultural order. Therefore, issues of social and cultural order bring to the forefront issues of social and moral/cultural control, of how society achieves the kind of conformity it needs. Sociologists typically think of this issue as the problem of social control.

Janowitz talks about "social control," by which he means voluntary control, and opposes it to "coercive control" (Janowitz, 1976). Gusfield (1957) refers to assimilative versus coercive reform categories.

Whether it be coercive or voluntary, the over-emphasis on "control" comes from a perspective attributed to Thomas Hobbes which sees man as sinful, man's life as "nasty, brutish and short," and a "war of all against all" as the problem of the day.*

The picture is perhaps more balanced if one recognizes that human beings not only need controls, but also need permissions. Perhaps societies are as much characterized by structures and belief systems which permit doing things as by those which prohibit doing things.**

Permission and Control

The emphasis upon control only, in the sociological literature, is somewhat one-sided. Perhaps it stems from a view of humanity which shows that we are not to be trusted - controls need to be placed upon us because of our inherently uncontrolled nature. But a stress upon this aspect of human nature leaves a related element untouched - we need permissions, too. Being more individualistically oriented, Western society focuses upon

---

*   While the Hobbsian perspective suggests "man" as aggressive, taking all from others, one can also see man as trepidatious, seeking many kinds of reassurances. "I'm ok, you're ok" is one such assurance. The permission/control perspective suggests they are linked.

** This point is important because, while permission and control form a duality (each somewhat opposed to the other), within each of the concepts itself are opposed elements. In the "Janowitzian" sense, control can have either the voluntary or the coercive aspect. Permission can be generated from self or others. In a sense, both permission and control have an internal and an external aspect, a point which shall be discussed later in the volume. Moral order typically is made up of both. It is also worth noting that controls (and permissions) can be either structural or cultural. The former are artifacts like law, rules, signs, barriers, and gateways of a formal, observable sort. The latter are beliefs, mental states, and dispositions like scorn, shame, guilt, etc.

the need for unity. Some collectively oriented societies - such as the Japanese - find the central problem to be one of liberating the individual (Woronoff, 1980). There, the central issue is permission. Rather than accepting either of these views as the only one, a sensible way to proceed is to assume that both problems - of permission and of control - are always present, and that society needs both. Different societies will need different combinations of permissions and controls.

This dichotomy is one of the key themes in the alcohol literature. Over our history American society has wavered back and forth, relatively speaking, between permission to drink and control of drinking. Both permission and control exist in the society at the same time, moving in relation to each other. One would be mistaken to think there was either a situation of full permission or full control. Rather, there is sometimes more of one than of the other.* During Prohibition, for example, Americans moved into a situation of greater social control, although there were many examples of permissions - speakeasies, bathtub beverages, etc. Social control was dominant. In contrast, the colonial period was one of relatively greater social permission. As will be noted in an upcoming chapter, the Pilgrims landed when they did, in part, because they had run out of beer! (But controls upon unwanted behavior were of course present, too).

Permission may have many sources and rationales, different from (but not necessarily opposite to) those which produce control. For example, increased permission may be engendered by economic variables (the cost of transporting whiskey made it the easiest form of grain to ship). Such economic considerations may play a heavy role. On the other hand, control may

* While the amount of control and permission is a central element, the location (or locus) of control and permission is a different, and important, dimension. Locus of control can be in the individual, or in the society. Regardless of where it is, however, it can be in greater or lesser amounts.

come from a desire to preserve one's status, as Gusfield (1963) suggests, rather than only from a desire to control alcohol itself.

However, permission and control should not be viewed as two ends of a continuum. A high position on one dimension does not necessarily mean a lower position on the other. Rather, they are two linked dimensions in the shape of a +. That is why the idea of permission versus control is so appealing. Permission can increase while control is high. One can have a high control/high permission society with respect to alcohol or anything else. This point is implicitly made by Bell (1960) when he asserts that Americans have more rules and morality, and more freedoms, than many other nations. Hence, rather than a high/low continuum there are four permission/control possibilities - high/high, low/low, high/low, and low/high. It might prove illuminating to give some thought to the ways in which permission and control interact within the society in general and with respect to alcohol in particular. This approach yields a four-fold table showing the intersections of permission and control vectors, and regions of varying combination of permission and control values.

Figure 1:
The Intersection of Permission
and Control Values

Level of Permission   Level of Control

                            Low   High

Low

High

For an analytic use of this table, see Figure 2.

A Cyclical Approach

As suggested by the value-conflict perspective, attitudes toward alcohol follow a cyclical pattern. One or another of the "cells" becomes dominant at various points in time, as permission waxes and wanes and as control waxes and wanes. Perhaps not strangely, it is very similar to the shift between "sensate" and "insensate" emphases in society which Sorokin developed (1941), and between the "ascetic" and "hedonistic" poles developed by Myerson (1940) (although Myerson seems completely unaware of Sorokin's work). It also links to the local/cosmopolitan distinction which has been developed by Gouldner (1957, 1958) to the aristocratic/egalitarian polarity used by Welter (1975) and applied by some in alcohol studies, as well as to the "dry" and "wet" polarities developed by the political system itself.

A value conflict perspective suggests adding ideas that (1) these dimensions are independent of each other, and (2) these central tendencies have a large variance. Thus, in a period characterized by one dimension, the other dimension is still present. After looking at liquor control elections, Gusfield (1963, p. 161) points out that there is a close balance between "dry" and "wet" forces. In some 12,000 elections between 1947 and 1959, where liquor was an issue, only 10 percent resulted in any change. Of that group, 45.3 percent went from wet to dry, and 54.7 percent went from dry to wet. Probably there were a minority of voters involved, as is generally suggested by political analysts, and more specifically by Stegh in a study of temperance in Ohio (Stegh, 1975).*

---

*   It is often surprising that in areas where the country thinks there is a "clear" consensus, the election results are rather closer than perceptions suggest. In the area of geographic mobility, for example, of American men at the end of their careers, it appears that about 58 percent had moved from the place where they grew up. This proportion is very close to 50/50 and quite different from what "everybody knows" is true, viz., that "most" people move.

Conclusion

The value conflict perspective - here the contest between social permission and social control - is a useful one for looking at the development of and change in approaches toward alcohol in American society. It sees any behavior (social or personal) as, in effect, the result of competing value commitments. A social policy, for example, must satisfy some permission and some control "forces." The weight of those views and their balance over time due to internal and external pressures, and thus behaviors and attitudes, are in a posture of continual and mutual adjustment. Such a dualistic theme is in fact present, though in other vocabulary, in current alcohol analyses. Before looking at the specific periods of alcohol history, however, it is important to look at the symbolic meaning of alcohol in American society.

CHAPTER THREE

CONTROL, AMERICAN SOCIETY, AND ALCOHOL

With its emphasis on the sanctity of the individual, issues of personal control are very important in Western culture and ultimately rest upon questions of whether or not the individual has control over his own soul. One example of non-western orientation is found in Japan.

> "The dominant image of what happens after death is that one 'enters' the 'cosmos,' stays there for a time, and then gradually fades away and disappears. ... The cosmos is created by preserving the harmony and security of the small group ... And because the cosmos eliminates individual differences and includes no transcendental agent, there can be no last judgement after death. No one goes to heaven just as no one goes to hell .... Thus, one important characteristic of modern Japanese people is a relatively weak consciousness of symbolic immortality for the individual ...." (Lifton, Kato and Reich, 1979, pp. 25-27).

Control in American History

When Thorner (1973) traces some of the attitudes toward alcohol back to the Protestant Ethic, he perhaps does not go far enough. He emphasizes the Protestant focus on realizing the goals of an ordered life. What also needs to be emphasized is the fundamental problem in Protestant life - that of permission (free will) versus control (predestination). The fact remains that there is major uncertainty about whether or not the individual does in fact have control over his future life in the form of his soul. On the one hand he has "permission" in the form of free will to do what he likes; on the other, this may or may not affect his celestial destination.

Essentially, predestination is the concept of man's character as fixed (that is, a man's character is fixed) and unalterable. Thus, the fundamental hope in America is not for geographic mobility or social mobility (important as those are in a secular sense) but rather for character (or soul) mobility. The social ladder is Jacob's ladder. Whatever the permissions granted in this life, the "final" decision has already been made, and cannot be influenced. It is in this precise sense that Americans have lots of questions about genetic determination, not so much because it has racial overtones (at this moment in time), but rather because it is a biological analogue to predestination, and implies lack of control. The matter of control of one's soul was always fudged somewhat. Beecher apparently felt that man's bad actions could keep him out of heaven, while good actions could only prepare him to receive grace. Still, this idea represents more freedom than might be strictly allowed by predestination terms, and becomes important in the move to control the bad actions resulting from drink (Winkler, 1972). Secular life becomes in some sense a "test" of inner character and the presence of grace.

However, there is naturally a great desire to find out what the "test" showed. On the pass/fail system of life, one is desperate for his grade, or any little indication that one might have passed or failed. Worldly success, as Weber (1956) suggested, can provide that indication.

Perhaps this issue had special meaning in American society. For hundreds of years - until the Reformation - European social structure was Catholic in origin. One might say Protestantism was an intruder ethic upon the Catholic scene. By contrast, in American society

Protestantism came first and the Catholic ethic was the intruder ethic. American society was founded by Protestants, and remained essentially Protestant until the big immigrations of the mid-19th century (Hudson, 1961). Protestant orientations toward individualism in relation toward God and local and independent organization of the church (it might be called decentralization, versus the hierarchical organization of the Catholic Church) articulated well within the new land. Individualism did not provide any kind of structure to fall back upon in times of personal uncertainty. In some sense, the government reflected and mirrored the church structure - independent, limited, and distant. Whatever control of fate the individual thought he had, the Protestant origin of the country, with its accompanying ethos, emphasized.

Early America - Calvinist/Protestant America - stressed individualism and individual control. However important that control was in day to day interaction, there was that fundamental uncertainty about whether one controlled one's fate after death through one's actions in life. The uncertainty which resulted runs like a "fault" through the American character, a line along which stress and concerns gather, and at which social and cultural forces erupt. It makes the problem of control especially important as a theme in American history, and in particular, the problem of internal control. It is certainly true that social control is a problem in all societies. Often the focus of that problem is external elements - governments, churches, bosses, seeking to tell one what to do. For American society, especially at the beginning, external controls were few. The main problem was self control, and fear that lack of self control might lead to revelations about one's inner character, and perhaps, that one was "damned."

As Stinchcombe (1965) points out, the founding culture of a social organization has an enduring if not indelible effect on the subsequent patterns within that social organization. Thus, the point about the founding ethos of American society is more than a simple specification of a sequence of cultural perspectives. It is a point about dominant and subdominant cultural emphases - which set of orientations might come to define American society, and which ones, coming later (in this case, Catholicism, among others) would have to adjust.*

Ambivalence and Alcohol

Issues of permission and control, therefore, are central to the American character, perhaps more so than for other societies because of the fundamental uncertainty about how much permission one has and how much control one can exercise.

Initially (as just discussed), the control issues focused upon religious matters. Over time, however, secular manifestations became a part of the picture. Secular uncertainty mirrored religious uncertainty. As an open society, America was the land of opportunity. But the other side of opportunity was uncertainty. Individuals were uncertain whether they could get ahead, or if they began to be successful whether they would stay successful. While the potential sacred significance of success added an extra dimension to the concern about it, uncertainty about secular success itself was enough to cause anxiety and concern. The very openness of society that was the occasion for hope was also the occasion for worry.

American society is therefore ambivalent society. On the one hand there is openness, opportunity, lack of fixed structure and independence. One could say there are supplies of permissions. Along with these permissions is a substantial amount of uncertainty.

On the other hand, there are a large number of controls. Early in the history of the United States there were controls on freedom itself for blacks, and substantial limitations on the rights of women. While openness might characterize the country as a whole, within specific communities intolerance often was more

---

* As yet, not much is known about the historical sequencing of cultural elements and how social units absorb and process them.

characteristic. From the Salem witch trials to the anti-Catholic "Protestant Crusade" (Billington, 1938), to the activities of Joe McCarthy in the 1950's, the manifestation of intolerance, racism, sexism, and generally negative groupthink have been a part of the American story.

Ambivalence has played a part in the alcohol story as well. Room (1976) notes that ambivalence is seen as a primary causal element in alcohol problems. Perhaps drink is one way to resolve the conflicting and contradictory pressures which are present in society. There is not only conflict between permissions and controls, but uncertainty about the meaning of permission and control. What does independence mean if one can find a job? What does control mean if one's fate has already been decided?

Ambivalence, therefore, has two senses, each of which can apply to the history of alcohol in America. One of them focuses upon uncertainty, and sees alcohol as a way to resolve uncertainties. Another sense emphasizes conflict, conflict between permission to drink and control of drinking. In effect, there are two sets of norms, each contradicting the other. It is this point that Meyerson was pursuing when he he sought to explain why women and Jews have different patterns of drinking from men and non-Jews. He uses ideas of social tradition (to avoid alcohol) and social pressure (to use alcohol) (Meyerson, 1940, p. 17).

Alcohol As Metaphor

Alcohol is the perfect (and the perfectly unique) arena in which to look at problems* of social and moral order in America because it is thought of as both the instance and the indicator of them. Perhaps no other "artifact" within American society simultaneously embodies problems of "order" in more concrete and

---

* "Problems" in this context do not mean "social problems" but rather issues - stresses, fissures - in the fabric of social order.

symbolic ways. While interesting in its own right, is also symbolic of matters involving permissions and control.

Gusfield (1963), for example, suggests that the temperance movement became an abstinence movement largely to put the new 19th century immigrants (who were largely Catholic and wet) at a moral disadvantage with respect to the "native" WASP population. In this sense, control of alcohol, however much merit the issue has on its face, has deeper and more transcendent meaning. Because of its specific association with problems of control and loss of control, it becomes a useful conduit through which more generalized concerns about control, and control impulses, can be exercised.

Another example of this tendency was the association, especially in the 19th century, between alcohol and poverty, especially for males. "Demon rum" was the enemy. For women, there was the old school's adage "smoking leads to drinking; drinking leads to sex; and sex leads to the gutter." This relationship was not merely an observed occurance, but was cast in causal terms - *viz.*, excessive drinking was a cause of poverty. Hence, one might reason, control of drinking would not only control specific problems associated with alcohol abuse, but would control poverty as well.*

---

*   Doubtless this argument seems strange to the modern reader. Part of the scientific problem is specifying the time order of drinking and poverty, as well as having proper data. But another part of the problem lies in loose definition - poverty then, as now, means so many different things that it is almost impossible to think scientifically about it. There are those today who believe that the provision of money cures poverty, by definition since for those individuals poverty is often <u>defined</u> as the absence of money, and only that. If in an earlier time one defined poverty as weakness as character, and alcohol use represented such a weakness, then its control would, in some sense, solve the problem.

This line of thinking suggests a "two-level assumption," i.e., that discussions about alcohol always operate at two levels: (1) the personal and the social control of alcohol itself, and (2) control in the society at large.* Whenever alcohol is discussed, I assume the discussion (or the attitude) has some "face" merit as well as merit as a "social" indicator. What people have to say about things always has wider meaning, and broader import. Talking about welfare recipients, for example, rarely refers just to the narrow number of actual recipients, but reflects the speaker's sense of the values of equity, family orientation, and the proper role of government. So, too, dispositions toward alcohol are indicative of orientations toward control, and toward permission as well.

Conclusion

Alcohol, therefore, has special meaning in American society, because problems of control and permission are especially central. The religious values (Calvinism) which founded this country were, as Max Weber (1956) has suggested, especially powerful here. The central features of the Protestant Ethic took root in American soil. These features - predestination and indications of salvation through worldly success - were the special locus of control problems in American society. On the one hand, predestination raised questions about the amount of control one actually had over his own life. On the other, there was the corrosive uncertainty about what material success might indicate. It could be a sign of sacred status; on the other hand, it could be lost, thus revealing that all along the individual had been damned. To some readers this discussion might sound a bit arcane, yet status uncertainty, problems of control, and other more civil and secular manifestations

---

*   Looking at alcohol as symbolic is nothing new. Jellinek (1977) points out that alcohol has been "representing" something for many years. Blood, friendship, etc., are among the most common symbols. The use of alcohol in religious ceremonies and in bonds of friendship are also ubiquitous.

of these concerns would ring a familiar bell. In a society with such social-psychological concerns as central issues, alcohol control would have a special place.

And, indeed, it does. Alcohol use has been the subject of two constitutional amendments, something which gives it a unique and special place in the history of American social policy, and is proof positive of its special place in American social concern.

This focus on alcohol is both direct and symbolic. Alcohol is of direct concern because, as a drug, its ingestion often directly causes problems of control of the individual in question. Like the automobile, its use is dangerous to self and dangerous to others, and needs to be controlled. Like the automobile, it enjoys wide permission so the problems of control exist within a context of permission.*

Alcohol control, like controls of car and handgun, serves symbolic functions as well. Discussing them allows one to discuss, almost in pantomime, deeper and more pervasive issues of permission and control in American society. Alcohol chemically enhances permissions and relaxes controls; the automobile does this physically, through its ability to move quickly over space, and the handgun does this psychologically, through its status as an "equalizer" and protector. Each of these products embodies and symbolizes permission/control problems. Perhaps for this reason each of them has something of a special status in American society, and each is routinely and historically the focus of battles over permission and control.

---

*   It would be possible to do a similar "history" with respect to cars and handguns. Alcohol certainly has the the longest history to inspect. If one looked at the others, however, the central argument here, that they occupy a central place in America's struggle with issues of permission and control should apply as well. Hence, one should find similarities in the historical cycle of policy and perspective toward them, too.

This history of alcohol attitudes in the United States is certainly a representation of a range of permission/control battles. It has moved through several phases in which orientations and dispositions toward alcohol have shifted, but the central issues of permission and control remain the same. It is to an exploration of these phases that we now turn.

CHAPTER FOUR

HISTORICAL PERIODS IN THE PERMISSION/CONTROL BALANCE

If one looks over the history of American society from a permission/control perspective, the expectation would be that at different historical junctures there would be different "packages" of permission/control combinations. (The four-fold table presented in Figure 1 could be a guide here). Some periods of history might be characterized by high permission, high control. At other times, low permission/low control might be the most salient characteristic. Figure 2 illustrates a "periodization" of American alcohol history, using Gusfield's (1967) categories of moral statuses - the repentant drinker, the sick drinker, and the enemy drinker. To them I have added a fourth and contemporary category - the responsible drinker. The proposed periods are outlined in Figure 2. It is important to stress that the periodization is a rough one, and not a set of dates cast in stone. Rather, they are meant to be suggestive and illustrative of major foci during particular historical epochs. A second point worth stressing is that the "central tendency" involved in periodization has considerable variance to it as well. Hence, no one should be misled into thinking that during a particular period everyone was characterized in this way. Surely there were subgroups with differing opinions and orientations, who have come from different and antithetical backgrounds. Indeed, nowhere would this be more likely true than American society, diverse and heterogeneous as it is. Yet the presence of variance and diversity should not prevent attempts at generalization, although they do make such attempts more hazardous.

Figure 2
Illustrative Patterns of Drinking Attitudes as They Relate to Levels of Permission and Control
(after Gusfield)

		Control	
Permission		Low	High
	Low	Repentant Drinker 1620-1820	Sick Drinker 1930-1960
	High	Enemy Drinker 1820-1931	Responsible Drinker 1960-

One might also expect, as the permission/control balance changes, additional shifts in the type of permissions and controls (from voluntaristic to coercive, for example) and in the locus of control (from the individual to the state, for example). As each of the periods is discussed, suggested changes in these areas will be mentioned.

Change in the permission/control balance is a dynamic process, operating, perhaps, a little like supply and demand. An increase in the "supply" of permissions (through ideas like freedom and independence, for example) might "demand" more controls; alternatively, increased supplies of controls may generate an increased demand for more permissions. Important here is the relationship of time to these factors. At any moment in time, increased permission might be associated with decreased controls, or at least the permission/control ratio might be changed. A similar result would occur if controls were increased. On the other hand, over time the relationship might be positive, with additional supplies of permissions carrying forth additional controls, and more controls creating the demand for more permissions. What is important to stress here is the dynamic interaction, over time, which forms new combinations of values we all hold and to which we are committed.

Figure 3
Provisional Graph, Rise and Fall of Permission and Control of Alcohol, American Society, 1620-1970

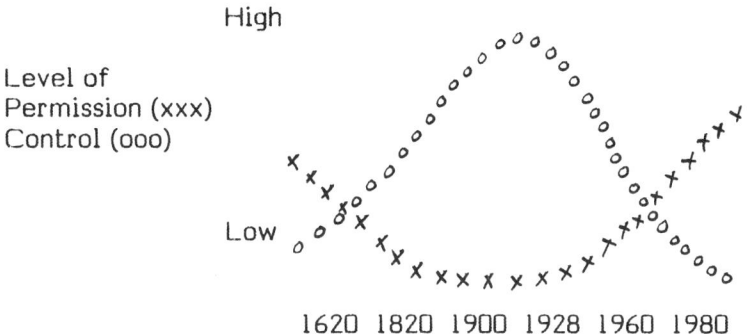

Level of
Permission (xxx)
Control (ooo)

High

Low

1620 1820 1900 1928 1960 1980

The Repentant Drinker

During the early years, American society was moderate on permission and low on control, with respect to alcohol, and the repentant drinker was the norm. Drinking was part of life, neither encouraged nor discouraged. The only thing which was discouraged was the "excessive use of beverages."

Lender makes the point that the image of restrictive "puritan" attitudes is unfounded (Lender, 1973). Rather, the puritan attitude was one of "social control," to use Janowitz's (1976) term. It was intoxication, rather than drinking, that was disapproved. Furthermore, and perhaps more important with respect to the way the word "puritan" has come to be used, there was no moral excitement about the matter. It seems to have been treated as a normal, natural part of life and that, within limits, was that.

The limits were the parameter-crossing behaviors of permission norms, which resulted in intoxication and, perhaps, the pillory. However, this excess was also seen as just that, and not as something which represented anything more. After the Revolution, social control appears to have loosened even more (Winkler, 1968).

It is difficult to imagine how fully integrated into the society liquor had become. People drank at breakfast, lunch, and dinner. People drank at all social occasions. In fact, people drank all the time for almost any reason. The high point was reached in the period of 1800-1830, with the amount of yearly consumption averaging 6.9 gallons of absolute alcohol per person of drinking age (15+)! That proportion is 150 percent more than the alcohol consumption rate in 1975! (Rorabaugh, 1979, Table A1.2, p. 233).

The Enemy Drinker

As the "high" consumption period of the 1820-30 period reached a peak, forces were developing which called forth greater controls. As might be expected, these forces were of different qualities and characters, and as is probably true in most situations of cultural change, it was the combination of stimuli, working in more or less unacknowledged concert, which began to produce results. As I discuss the factors it should be emphasized that there is no special order of importance, but they are divided into cultural factors (the effect of ideas) and structural forces (the effect of actions and artifacts).

On the cultural side, the heady ideas of independence, always present in American society, were loosened by the success of the revolution. At some point, more control is called for. The influence of independence ideology was noted in the field of aging by Fischer's (1978) work. He saw the rising power of that concept as responsible for the development of disteem of the older adult. A different effect here, in the alcohol area, might be to exacerbate the subordinate control portion of the permission/control duality, and generate demand for additional control.

A second cultural feature which is not directly related to alcohol, but might have a reinforcing effect, is the potential need for increased controls in the system due to the presence of slavery. Surely the increased climate of independence sorely tried those who were not free. A number of abolitionist efforts had begun, and at least for a portion of the society (the South) increased controls might well have been welcomed.*

On the structural side, technological and social changes were occurring that also stimulated the desire for more controls. Certainly the level of alcohol consumption was rising, and problems associated with a high consumption period were rising too. This trend was exacerbated and stimulated by a change in the available beverages. Beer, wine and cider had been typical; now hard liquor was becoming popular as farmers changed their agricultural products into booze. (Recall the "Whiskey Rebellion"!). Then, too, the increased mechanization of the society and the developing of industrialization created a pressure to control drinking. It is one thing to be drunk while using a hoe; it is another to be drunk while using power equipment in a factory. Mechanization created the need for a more disciplined work force, because power-driven machines are a lot less forgiving than hand operated ones.

Associated with early industrialization was something of an increase in cooperative effort. While nothing like the collective integration required on an assembly line, there were still interdependencies in which the work of one employee depended upon or impacted that of another in a way that was not true of the solitary farmer. Hence an additional push for increased sobriety. It is one thing if a farmer harms

---

* The suppression of an entire people requires both manifest violence and the threat of violence. This situation can be seen in the South Africa of the latter part of the 20th century. For the South, associations with violence and alcohol were a feature of that culture into this century, according to Arthur Krock (1968).

his own livelihood; it is something else if a fellow worker harms yours.

Demographic changes were occuring too which may have stimulated the desire for more controls. Immigration and urbanization were occurring, creating centers of non-WASP (and hence, "non-traditional") Americans. Singly each would have been important. Their simultaneous occurrence increased their impact. The urban place was something of a permissive arena, and as it grew, controls were needed to counter what might be seen as its growing influence. Part of this influence was related to the influx of foreign labor, such as the Irish and the Germans, who were different from the population groups who had founded this country in religion and nationality. Their presence, as Gusfield has suggested, called for some controls.

Throughout the early period of "enemy drinker," many Protestant churches took it upon themselves to vent their indignant contempt upon the idle, immoral public inebriate (Linsky, 1970). The link between alcohol and other more important moral characteristics was beginning to be forged. The tone of attitudes was one of law and morality (Globetti, 1973), laced with the ambivalence and confusion that always characterize change. There was also the beginning of the religious fanaticism which emphasized inner control (Thorner, 1953; Stroupe, 1975).

The early period can be seen as stretching from the turn of the century up through the Civil War, with a second period beginning after the Civil War and running to Prohibition. According to Turner, few of the prohibition organizations and movements survived the Civil War (Turner, 1972). They did begin again afterwards, however, which is a tribute to the power and vigor of these social ideas, in that they remained undaunted by the Great Rebellion. They flourished and came to a head with Prohibition.

The characteristic of this period was the view of

the drinker as outcast and outlaw.* This designation, of course, is completely consistent with the idea of the drinker as enemy. It is most handy to have a theological and moral enemy also be the legal enemy. This designation is linked with an emphasis on internal and external control, and repression through penal management and government intervention. The enemy/outlaw designation makes this kind of coercive control (using governmental authority to back up voluntary control) quite possible. The outlaw label permits and justifies increments in the use of force.

Apparently these measures have some effect. The per capita consumption of alcohol of drinking age Americans (age 15+) dropped steadily throughout the period, from a peak of 7.10 U.S. gallons (of absolute alcohol!) in 1810 to 2.4 gallons in 1915, or a drop of 66 percent! (Rorabaugh, 1979, Table A1.2, p. 233).

This period was the high tide of American Protestantism. Winthrop S. Hudson, in his masterful survey of the history of American Protestantisms, comments:

> The whole mood and spirit of the country, however, seemed so indelibly Protestant that in the end it was confidently believed, all minority groups would be either 'assismilated' or 'Americanized.' It was with some such conviction in mind that Leonard W. Bacon was able to report in 1897 that "the Catholic advance in America has not been, comparatively speaking, successful. . . " (Hudson, 1961, p. 126).

* Each phase, to some extent, lays the groundwork for the next. The designation of the drinker as the enemy, and later the outlaw, provided intellectual beginnings for the adoption of the drinker as sick, much as the criminal himself has been labeled as sick.

These were only some of the tensions in the system. Protestantism, although it would score more successes, was giving way. Hudson comments:

> These outward indications of Protestant strength and well-being, however, were deceptive. They represented little more than the high tide of a Protestant advance which had been carried forward by an accumulated momentum from the past, and the momentum was largely spent. In spite of the busyness of the churches the halcyon years of the two decades bridging the turn of the century actually marked the end of an era (Hudson, 1961, pp. 126-127).

It was not all that peaceful and harmonious, however, even with lower alcohol consumption. In his biography, Arthur Krock talks about the need of a southern sheriff to kill three brothers who became violent after drinking too much, and then comments:

> This wholesale instance of justifiable homicide was not unusual in the South of my boyhood. Its source, the dangerous combination of the Southerner and whiskey, was a major reason these communities voted dry and were - as many remain - steadfast advocates of national prohibition (Krock, 1968, p. 9-10).

Prohibition was the furthest point this high tide reached. Perhaps the turning point of "that old time religion" came, symbolically, when Clarence Darrow defeated William Jennings Bryan in a trial in a small Tennessee town, in a trial about the right to teach evolution. Repeal followed shortly thereafter.

The "enemy" period was a powerful one, and left an important mark upon American society. Its repressiveness and controlling themes were added to Puritan ones, and transformed the more moderate (though not wildly joyous) Puritans into pillars of repression, an unfounded image.

The increasing number of controls sifting through the society in what Hudson calls the period of "shaping a Protestant America" were perhaps generative of the need for more release. At least one place this release was found was in the many revivals and great awakenings which characterized this period. A sudden born-again experience (characteristic of many periods, including today's) could provide a release from a prison of controls otherwise too confining. In a sense, perhaps there is an inverse relationship (at least in that period) between release through alcohol and release through religious experience. It may be that when these forces of release become opposed each to the other, societal tension rises. It may also be that this is why so many religions have enfolded ardent spirits into their ceremony - perhaps seeking this way to control them. At the same time, some religions have prohibited them as an alternate means of control. But, increasingly, the enemy perspective diminished and a more health-related perspective began to develop. When the doctors of divinity becmame disenclined, the ministers of medicine moved in.

The Sick Drinker

The Pilgrim's Progress of moral passage is never smooth. Perhaps the "enemy drinker" period ended with repeal, but "ending" is a concept which has no explicit meaning in an historical analysis. It is more a waxing and waning, with different hues appearing as the mixture shifts. We can tell day and night easily enough, but dawn and dusk are harder to specify.

The same is true here. The dusk of the enemy drinker looks a lot like the dawn of the sick drinker. Times were changing. As early as Benjamin Rush [1785] (1934), medical people had been interested in alcohol and its properties from a medical viewpoint. While Protestantism waned, secular substitutes were needed for intellectual and moral structures. During the first part of this century - that is, during the end of the enemy drinker period - the sickness mentality was taking hold in many spheres. We should not think it was just alcohol which was coming under medical interpretation. Freud was arriving on the scene, and in a sense he began the transition from the "enemy" - drinker, poverty stricken, and criminal - to the "sick" - drinker, poverty stricken, and criminal.

The first step in this transition was the shift from religious to psychological interpretation, from religious to mental illness, from sin to schizophrenia. In the early days of the psychiatric profession, psychiatrists were called alienists because they dealt with people somehow alienated from society. Later the term "psychiatrists" came into use, and, yet later, biological elements came to play a growing role in the medical thinking about alcohol - stimulated, no doubt, by the observable physiological effects of much poor quality stuff during the Prohibition era. In an overall sense, we have moved from approbation to abolition to alienation to antabuse.

The period, then, between the turn of the century and World War II, just about 100 years after the last shift, saw another series of shifts, which began to move the "permission curve" up and the "control curve" down. Urbanization and the rise of cities might have been one factor. A second might have been the international experience of the first world war. The question of "how are you going to keep them down on the farm after they have seen Paree?" becomes of more than academic interest. A third factor was cultural - the decline of Protestantism (or of forces of control represented by 19th Century Protestantism). A fourth factor was the availability of a medical (or psycho/medical) theoretical framework which could be used to sustain interpretations of illness. Furthermore, one cannot discount the "heady" atmosphere which follows victory. "The roaring 1920s" followed victory in Europe much as the 1810-30 period followed victory over England.

Much as diagnoses were moving to internal bases, using the medical model, so were mechanisms of control. In the 1800s we saw the rise of machinery and the "need for a disciplined work force," and in the 1900s we saw the rise of the white collar "trades" with their somewhat greater emphasis on internal, self-control. From a control point of view, white collar people (especially white collar professionals) may be similar to farmers - much of their success depends upon being self-starters. In any event, white collar occupations grew from 17.62 percent in 1900, to 36.61 percent in 1950, to 48.3 percent in 1970.* To the extent that white collar workers are professional, they are more likely to be self-supervised and, thus, demand and get greater freedoms (permissions).

As a sixth factor, we should note the rise of egalitarianism as represented by the inclusion of women in voting. While this effort was not "all that was needed" by any means, it was reflective of a somewhat greater participation of women in the society in a formal way. And when women asked society to "blow some my way," it was reflective of greater permission across the board. Perhaps the highlight of the rising permission, or at least one high point, came in the 1920s.**

Seventh, the media was a factor due to the increasing impact of the media itself and its representatives - stars and glamour people (Linksy, 1970, Cahalen and Cisin, 1976) Their modeling and example

* The first two figures are derived from The Statistical History of the United States (Fairfield Publishers), Series D 72-122, p. 74. The last figure is from the City County Data Book, 1972.

** The influence of women came not only here, but in temperance organizing as well. It may be that this confluence directed social change effort from suffrage to "dry" legislation, two powerful elements. This may have left the interpretation of alcohol abuse to the intrapersonal dimension, with the external dimension having been "used up," as it were.

doubtless affected the populous at large, although it is hard to specify or quantify this in any way. One point is obvious, however: movies, radio, and telephone tied the society together in a way never before anticipated, especially when one thinks that when Arthur Krock was a boy, very little of what we define as modern conveniences existed.

These changes supported and were supported by another factor - the car. The car embodied greater permission, if only in the form of freedom from scrutiny and direct control.* Like professionalization, the car required internal controls because the driver, and anyone with him, was freed from the "eyes of the street" which served to keep people under a form of social control.** The rumble seat, however, could be physically taken away from prying eyes, and under those conditions only the internal norms could serve to control activities on lover's lane.

*   We cannot get into the whole set of ideas about mobility in its geographical sense here, but - as mentioned before - it is crucial to understanding the American character and might be crucial to understanding alcohol values as well. Americans have fled controls - by moving over distances, by running away, and by psychological means. Alcoholism might be considered a sort of mental mobility equivalent to geographical mobility. In any event, the flight from control has been a very important element in American mythos and fact. The car provided such mobility and freedom, in ways never before imagined. As mentioned, Phillip Slater (1970) explores this perspective in some detail.

**   Like professionalism, over time the auto creates the need for more external and coercive control because of the problems created by those few who are not compelled by internal controls. Careless drivers - like professionals who abuse their position, for instance - force controls upon us and limit our freedom.

Directly or indirectly, this combination of factors tended to support the medical models of illness in general and "sick ideas of alcoholism" in particular. It was a similar confluence of social and cultural forces 100 years earlier which had led to the rise of control. Now different forces lead to a rise in permission.

It should be underscored, however, that the transcendence of the therapeutic and the suzerainty of the supportive was not uniquely focused upon alcoholism. With the passage of the Social Security Act in the 1930s, the poor were provided caseworkers to assist them in their functioning, and the work of Virginia Robinson (1930), who was highly influential in social work, provided psychological interpretation of many of the cases.

As expected, the period of the sick drinker began even as the period of the enemy drinker was in its heyday, and the actual changes in social structure - repeal, for example - came after the value change was well underway.

The Responsible Drinker

Is it still in the period of the enemy drinker, or has another period begun? Though the timing may be problematic, we should theoretically be due for a period of high permission/high control. As times passes, the higher permission of the enemy drinker period should create conditions which call for higher control consistent, for a time, with higher permission. For example, we now have M.A.D.D., Mothers Against Drunk Driving. And there are now sharp increases in the Anti Driving and Drinking campaigns. In 1985, the Detroit Tiger Baseball Club banned full strength beer at the ballpark, using "low alcohol" beer instead. And a nationally marketed low alcohol beer had already been made available. A new period has begun and could be called "enlightened hedonism". As many will recognize, this phrase comes from the very end of Meyerson's seminal essay on ambivalence. It is a tribute to his wisdom that, so many years ago, he was able to recognize the essential elements of this newer period.

Extending the terms of the drinker labels which Gusfield uses, one could label this period one of the "controlled drinker" or the acceptable, moderate, responsible drinker.

While drinking is widespread, we are nowhere near the high level of consumption which characterized our earlier history. While drinking is accepted, it appears also that the medical model - and the illness psychology - has some limitations which cannot be ignored especially those involving youth and automobiles. These are situations where "sick" seems not to be an appropriate description for the person involved.

A large factor might be the recognition (again) of the high involvement of alcohol in fatalities, especially vehicular manslaughter. The car initially forced greater permission, and now forces greater control. The road and the car present the same type of interdependent situation seen earlier in American society by the development of the need for a disciplined work force. It has the same two variables - use of heavy machinery and the development of high interdependency. It thus presents potential danger to the operator, and especially to others. The expansion of the national defense interstate road system during the 1950s may have been the key element in crystallizing this situation, bringing vehicle deaths into sharper focus, and "a death in the family" (Agee, 1971) became interpreted as alcohol related and pressed the societal demand for more control. Thus, the high permission society creates situations which result in the need for more controls.

There were other factors in society which suggested the need for more controls, especially following the 1960s. Then, urban unrest brought forth some instances of military intervention in American cities and created a climate supportive of more controls. Also, the use of drugs other than alcohol moved out of the lower class and the media elite into the general populace, especially among youth, which again made the need for controls more essential. Introduction of widespread tranquilizing drugs (e.g, Miltown) in the middle '50s led to a climate of acceptance regarding ingestion of mind altering drugs. The drug-taking "kids" of the 1960s must have been the suburban children of the '50s who had observed their parents in Levittown and Park Forest taking tranquilizing drugs. They simply carried it a step further. But alcohol still remained the drug of choice, although there was a great deal of uncertainty surrounding it.

A climate has now been created in which these drugs are an accepted part of American life. Alcohol "benefits" by this increased permission. The problem with drugs is one of overdose, and so the issue for the society is how to control and moderate drug intake. Similarly, the same general problem exists for alcohol - drinking is "ok," overdosing is not. We're back to 1810.

Cahalan and Cisin review some Harris poll findings:

> To sum up the present state of American attitudes and values concerning alcohol, events in our history reinforced by findings of recent surveys of the general public, lead to the conclusion that a large proportion of the American people are rather uneasy and misinformed about the subject of drinking and its consequences (Cahalen and Cisin, 1976, p. 87).

One might say, "So, what else is new?" but they go on to note that a policy of moderation (which they apparently favor) is hampered by this ambivalence:

> . . . . the general public will need to be well informed and to have confidence that they *can* (and should) keep their drinking within moderate limits (Cahalan and Cisin, 1976, p. 83).

They also note - and from our perspective quite significantly - that problem drinking occurs when controls are weak.

> National survey findings show that problem drinking is heavily dependent upon the individual's social supports and restraints. Thus, the highest rates of problem drinking are to be found among those who live within highly permissive or indifferent social environments, who live in large cities, who are psychologically alientated from middle class values and who are economically insecure.

As members of the alcohol researcher cadre, these are influential in setting and suggesting the norms and values of the govenment and populace. They are the more influential because of the ambivalence and confusion which exists here.* It is important that, while they are recommending increased social control, they are not recommending withdrawal of permission. In fact, they rather encourage moderate, controlled drinking.

We would be remiss to write an entire paper on attitudes toward alcoholism without discussing sex and sexual attitudes. Meyerson makes this explicit connection, and there is ample historical association between the two. One function of controlling female drinking, for example, might be (or might have been) to prevent a loosening of sexual controls which could lead to "complications." The attempt by men to use liquor to loosen social controls on sexual activity is well known. The old phrase about how to secure sexual compliance from women goes, "Candy is dandy but liquor is quicker." (No one, for example, has ever reported seeing couples driving down the road tossing empty boxes of candy out the window!) The point here is to stress the

---

* One might note that there have always been alcohol gurus who "knew" what was proper. The fact that social scientists have replaced ministers and that conventions have replaced the Chataqua is notwithstanding and simply a comment on the current idiom.

likelihood that control of alcohol - who drinks, how much is allowed, where and when people drink, etc. - is, in part at least, a way to control sexual activity. Greer (1984) comments, for example, about why adults so often exclude children from their activities:

> Adults cannot have fun while kids are around; kids must be "put down" first. Drinking and flirting, the principle expressions of adult festivity, are both inhibited by the presence of children (Greer, 1984, p. 3).

To the extent, then, that freedom from conception is more prevalent today than it has been, and to the extent that control of women's drinking has the function of controlling opportunities for conception, then these controls should now be loosened. Indeed, more women seem to be drinking (Cahalan and Cisin, 1976).

However, as these factors create greater freedoms, they also create demands for new controls. How can society control "drug abuse?" How can society control sexual activity now that an important inhibitor - for persons and society - is of much less importance? New norms and values will need to be developed and instituted. Because these activities, by nature, are more private than public, it is likely that voluntary control (as opposed to coercive) will be the mode chosen. And, paradoxically, the increase in women drinkers could be a move toward such control (a point discussed in the next chapter).

Whether or not this complex of factors is sufficiently powerful to move us from a sick drinker perspective to an enlightened, controlled drinker perspective is, of course, open to question. However, control of responsible drinking seems to parallel the problem of controls within society. The '60s may have represented a watershed of "permission," and it is likely that a period of increase of "control" is beginning.

Conclusion

In this section, an historical progression of modal approaches to alcohol in America has been suggested. As heuristic as these designations are, the usual caveats apply, *viz.*, that they are "ideal types," that there was variation within each period, that since each period gave birth to the next one, we would see some of the patterns yet to emerge in full flower early, that these simplifications are not the whole story, etc. But they remain helpful in at least sectioning off historical periods, and suggesting how cultural and structural change interacts with alcohol attitudes.

CHAPTER FIVE

LOCI OF PERMISSION/CONTROL

Levels of permission and control are not the only aspects worth understanding. We need to look at other aspects of the control system as well. First, there is the locus, or location, of control within the cultural system. Where exactly does the society think the control of goods and services is located? In some cases, as in the "capitalist" societies, the locus is (or thought to be) with the person, and so in this sense it is at the individual level. In terms of alcohol attitudes, these societies hold the view that it is the person himself who controls his drinking, and they hesitate to use external means on the drinker except in the extreme instance. Some say that in America, while we are willing to offer advice on any matter and even willing to tell people they have had too much to eat, we are unwilling to tell anyone they have had too much to drink. Alcohol abuse is a crucial problem within industry, abetted by the fact that the norms of control here operate on the level of the individual.

Alternatively, locus of control can be on the societal level. In this approach, control of alcohol (or anything else) is achieved through laws and administrative enforcement. Here, control is in the hands of the state. The individual is encouraged to follow state law on the subject. In Sweden, for example, laws against drinking and driving are much more severe than in the United States. Even now, various groups in America are pushing for stiffer controls.

Crucial Variables in the Locus of Permission/Control

This general history has spotlighted, from a permission/control perspective, some high points and shifts in the history of attitudes toward alcoholism. This perspective integrates and codifies an approach to looking at historical patterns, and additionally avoids the challenge so aptly formulated by Room (1976). It also links, at least conceptually, the shifts in permission/control equilibria in the alcohol field to more general conflict of the same type in the society at large.

More emerges than can be treated in a simple historical framework. Attention is needed which looks at elements in the historical periods, rather than the history itself. This "cross sectional" analysis highlights crucial variables that keep coming up again and again, but which could not be considered in depth by the emphasis on the longitudinal description. Furthermore, each variable represents a crucial axis of permission/control in the society at large, and this link can only be emphasized by looking at each variable specifically.

This chapter, therefore, examines seven dimensions or areas of conflict, each representing:

1) a crucial axis of the permission/control theme;
2) important elements in the history of alcohol attitudes;
3) a link between alcohol attitudes conflicts and permission/control conflicts in the society at large.

The seven areas of permission/control conflict are:

1) voluntary versus governmental
2) male versus female
3) collegial versus communal (familial)
4) drinking versus alcoholism
5) rationality versus non-rationality (fault versus no fault)
6) internal versus external
7) mastery versus drift.

The same kind of value-clash perspective has been used in presenting these conflicts as in the presentation of the permission/control dyad itself. Each of these juxtaposed arenas is the one which contains issues of permission/control conflict. But each is a locus of permission/control as well.

Voluntary Versus Government

Throughout the country's history, "voluntary" controls have alternated with "governmental" controls. One is non-coercive, the other invokes formal, legal mechanisms. Over the years, control of the production of alcohol and its consumption have both been the subject of voluntary and coercive elements. The Whiskey Rebellion is an early example of the use of governmental coercion. Prohibition is another. The use of government authority to insist that certain persons take antabuse to prevent drinking is a third example. In addition to Federal interest, we should mention the host of state regulations about the hours and days liquor and wine can be sold, the difference in alcohol amount in beers, the specification and change of legal drinking ages, the location of sales centers, and the availability of liquor licenses based on the number of "saloons" per capita.

On the other hand, we should not ignore the heavy volunteeristic aspect which has been and continues to be part of beverage control. Perhaps the most famous example is Alcoholics Anonymous, which was preceded by the Washingtonian Society, and before that by numerous moral exhortations, appeals, and taking "the pledge." Indeed, the whole temperance movement was heavily voluntary, although buttressed with successful legal incursions within states and localities.

And while it is not generally understood in this way, the radical change throughout the 19th century in the amount of alcohol Americans consumed is an example of voluntary control. By the turn of the 20th century, alcohol consumption in the United States had fallen to around 2 gallons per capita or less (Rorabaugh, 1979). Certainly the substantive goals of "prohibition" had largely been achieved even before the law was changed.

Within American society, the whole matter of govenmental control has been a sensitive issue. "Conservatives" generally have taken the anti-governmental, pro-voluntary position, and "liberals" take the more pro-government position. There are two important variations on this pattern, however, which may be important to consider - region and level of government.

One variation in the pattern of public/private structure occurs by region. In terms of region, as one moves from east to west there is a preference for the use of public institutions. That Harvard is on the Atlantic and Berkeley on the Pacific illustrates this point, within academic circles. It is also true of child welfare agencies - on the east coast there has been a history of private child caring agencies, such as the New England Home for Little Wanderers, while on the west coast the public sector has had a much more highly developed position with respect to this social service.

It is not clear why the society of the east decided to work through private structures and the west through public ones.* Because the lands were settled at different historical periods, the different temperament of the times may have been involved.

A second variation involves public/voluntary attitudes toward level of government. Generally, we suggest a mixed identifier pattern, with "conservative" and "liberal" labels being only poor proxies for attitudes toward governmental action once level is taken into consideration.

---

*   The picture, as always, is mixed. Stanford is on the west coast, too, and recently the east coast has begun to develop some public institutions.

Republicans tend to be locally pro-government action and nationally anti-government action, while Democrats tend to the reverse. The point becomes clear when one observes who supports better schools, parks, civic improvements, and takes a generally public-regarding political view - the middle class conservative group - but this is only true at the local level. Conversely, Democrats are more likely to support federal action and be less positive about these types of public expenditures at the local level.

Part of this difference may relate to the nature of the issues involved, and part, as Banfield and Wilson (1963) suggest, to the different views about the purpose of politics, as embodied in the public - versus the private - regarding view. At least from the start, though, it is not the same at each of the levels of government and traditional political labels seem less apt. Liberal and conservative citizens seek effective controls on alcohol abuse, whether it is voluntary, governmental, or a combination; whether it is local, state, or federal.

But American society overall has a preference, it seems, for the voluntary. Recent campaigns of a "public service" nature are appearing on television, urging citizens to avoid drinking and driving. Bumper stickers urging personal control of individual and family drinking appear ("American teenagers are dying for a drink!"). Substance abuse treatment centers are developing within the workplace. The alcohol abuser is in the process of being socially isolated, through voluntaristic means. Figures appear indicating how many people - family and friends - the abusive drinker negatively impacts. Within the therapeutic field, a movement to identify and assist the "adult child of the alcoholic" is burgeoning. And Americans are drinking milder beverages - more wine, and wine-based beverages, lower alcohol beer, etc. - without any legislation to that effect.

Historically, American society has swung back and forth between emphasis on government control and emphasis upon voluntary (or "social") control.* One aspect of the permission/control contest lies in the difficult roles of government and private realms in structuring this permission and control.

Men Versus Women

Gender plays an important role in alcohol matters. As Bacon comments, when spirits became available in significant quantities, drinking became a predominantly male, out-of-the-home activity (Bacon, 1967). The comment by Arthur Krock reflects male violence, not female, and the characters of western saloon life, as typified on Gunsmoke, were male except for a few women (like Kitty) who worked there.

Women have played an important role in alcohol control. The number of women involved in the temperance movement was large, especially after the Civil War. It might be a version of the egalitarian/aristocratic conflict (Welter, 1975) which permeated the period, except that here men were the aristocrats (they had the vote and all the fun) and women were the underclass. Along with blacks, they were not permitted the range of rights that men enjoyed.

In a sense, the relationship of women to drinking has changed over the years from personal abstinence and a generally negative view toward drinking (including a more active participation in the temperance movement - The Women's Christian Temperance Union!) to a more modern posture of joining men in drinking. From a functional point of view, the role of women and alcohol can be seen as a social control mechanism. In the immediate post-Civil War period, women sought to control male drinking through prohibition and negative attitudes toward drinking generally. This strategy then

*   This same issue is now appearing in the debate over firearms control. And the prohibition model is being explicitly explored. Kates (1984), for example, titles his chapter on this issue "Handgun Banning in the Light of the Prohibition Experience" and concludes that the success of "force" is limited.

changed as prohibition proved ineffective, to one in which women joined men in drinking, and, in this more modern pattern, sought to embrace alcohol within the family pattern in a more moderate way.

Women may have had something of an ally in this effort to control male drinking through organized religion. Religions have also sought to control (and sometimes prohibit) drinking. The Bible belt, for example, is also the moonshine belt. As more frequent church attenders, women's views may both define to some extent religious orientation, and they may also be more exposed to religious injunction and instruction.

What may be common here between the role of religion and the role of women is the concern about male violence. Arguably, male violence is a great world problem, whether that violence is manifest in an individual attack or armies locked in combat.

Male violence is destructive of individuals, systems and families. Its control is a central social task, to which many social institutions are devoted, directly and indirectly. Violence, especially personal physical attack, is exacerbated by alcohol, and hence, control of alcohol and drinking is, to some degree, control of violence. For women, fear of sexual attacks occurring "under the influence" is an important personal motivation. Such attacks may come outside marriage or inside marriage. Violence could be a factor in either case. But self protection is not the only motive here; the social goal or preventing or at least and tamping violence is an important, if latent part of women's "role."* For the

* The latent aspect of women's role in controlling male violence may extend to personally absorbing some of it if all else fails. It could be for this reason that attitudes and actions about spouse abuse and rape appear so tentative and are laced with victim blaming. In this context the idea that "she deserved it" takes on a new meaning, not that "she" was provocative or causal, as in the usual sense, but that she failed at a situational job assignment.

most part, this is also a role of religion, as well.*

The idea that drinking is somehow "male" and females have a role in trying to control that drinking has perhaps been an important component in causing American society, at least, to overlook female addiction. At an earlier point in time, when women and men indulged separately, "healing waters" were often consumed by women. One recent ad in a New England catalog offered "Florida Waters" - a 55 percent alcohol concoction which it was asserted has been used by women for 150 years for various ailments and by men a a shaving lotion! Certainly a versatile beverage.

One of the places where the battle of the sexes has been waged is in the area of alcohol. On the most concrete level, it has been about who drinks, who can drink, and who becomes violent when they drink.**

It is important to recall the two-level hypothesis, that alcohol processes always operate at a manifest and a latent level. Here the control of alcohol, drinking, and violence is just one part of the much larger issue of control and permission generally. As the locus shifts to women, controls increase. At the same time, permissions may decrease, as in the Prohibition period, or they may be neutral to positive, as in the modern period. Overall, permission and control is an aspect of the gender dimension of alcohol, with men representing or seizing greater permission and women representing or

---

* "For the most part" recognizes that at times religion is also violent and aggressive. The Crusades are but one example of religious armies.

** Walton notes that in the South the concern that black males would sexually attack white women was exacerbated by alcohol. Tennessee passed both dienfranchisement laws and prohibition laws in 1909 (Walton, 1970).

seizing greater control.*

Collegial Versus Familial

The location where drinking occurs represents another nexus of permission/control controversy. Society exerts control over drinking and the drinker. "Collegial drinking" refers to drinking with "buddies" or other men, often at a special place - a saloon or tavern - set aside for drinking. Naturally, special norms which increase permission are present there.

On the other hand, "familial drinking" refers to alcohol use within the family structure - with meals, but also at home in the presence of children and family. Familial drinking represents a greater element of control than "saloon" or "bar" drinking for several reasons: (1) One continues to have other responsibilities if one stays in the house; the "boys' night out" idea doesn't work in one's own house; (2) Spouses may restrain each other, to some degree; this is especially true of women restraining men; (3) The presence of children, and their needs and requests, tends to have a similar effect.** Both kinds of groups are powerful, and both exert an influence on behavior. Separate locations are important because the kinds of bonds generated by one mechanism tend to conflict with those generated by the other mechanism.

To a degree, therefore, the setting determines the permission control balance within it, and the patterns of drinking within a culture, will determine the nature and level of alcohol use. Cultures and societies which

* It may be this aspect of control, as opposed to punishment, which leads to the phenomenon of "mother blaming." This tendency apparently has not decreased in recent years (Caplan and Hall-McCorquodale, 1985).

** Note the previous quote by Germaine Greer. It should be understood that by familial I do not mean solitary drinking in one's house. Rather, we mean that the use of alcohol is an accepted part of the family's activity.

integrate drinking into the home pattern - familial drinking - should be less likely to have as many problems with alcohol as those in which drinking is segregated into collegial settings. Since collegial settings (with some exceptions in ethnically integrated settings) are characterized by a lack of ongoing responsibility for the separate individuals involved, the press toward permission is very heavy.

Collegial and familial settings also use different kinds of solidarity to achieve their goals. Historically these might be called the solidarity of similarity versus the solidarity of interdependence. Collegial settings involve people engaged in parallel process - separate individuals performing similar functions, in synchrony with each other, but not involved with each other.* Durkheim called the kind of cohesion generated by this type of interaction "mechanical solidarity" (1947). Amos Henry Hawley (1950) referred to its as a categoric group because all of the members were from the same or a similary category.

Alternatively, interdependence as is characterized by the family is called "organic solidarity" by Durkheim (1947), and a corporate group by Hawley. There the feeling of common bonds comes from the fact of mutual needs for each other, rather than from the sameness of function or role.

From a policy point of view, regulation of the setting involves regulation of the alcohol patterns. It is for this reason that states and localities pay special attention to the number of saloons and bars, their location, and their condition.

A variety of factors may influence a societal choice of location for drinking, factors which may interact with the functions just mentioned. A

* This observation is true of many American bars and saloons. Some neighborhood pubs and ethnic watering holes may be more characterized by interdependence only because people there see and interact with each other regularly.

geographically mobile society may have few or no familial locations (as in a military location). The nature of the beverage may influence its use, and the economics of beverage manufacture may influence the nature of the available beverages. But whatever the location, collegial and familial influences play a part in the total picture.

In sum, an integrated, familial setting is one in which permissions are limited and controls are present, at least with respect to drinking. The segregated, collegial setting is one in which controls are less present.* Changes over time in the settings in which drinking occurs are, at the same time, changes in the locus of permission and control, and in the relative balance of permission and control.

Drinking Versus Alcoholism

Another place where the permission/control conflict works itself out is intellectual in nature, and refers to the ways the whole matter is defined. On the other hand, the "drinking is permissive" definition sees alcohol as a usual part of life. While it may recognize problems, the central element of the definition is not "problem focused." As with other things which have dangerous aspects - fire, guns, cars - users are cautioned, but not prohibited from use, although there are usually some specific conditions set for their use.

---

* This observation may not obtain for oriental societies where the workplace may well be a "family" in many important senses. In Japan, for example, evening drinking is a part of the job - really, an extension of the workday - and is done by men in bars and restaurants. But, because of the structure of social permission/control in Japanese society, this setting is not "uncontrolled" (though it is high permission) in the same sense that it would be in American society. In fact, many bars have whiskey bottles with the names of regular customers in neat rows behind the bar.

Demon run, though, represents a different way of thinking about alcohol, a point of view, which is characteristic of high control, or the need for control. Demons need to be controlled, and the focus here is on the substance rather than on the user. Controlled drugs and substances are one example, and these need to be dispensed by a physician through a drug store. (Indeed, the essentially correct view that alcohol was a drug was one of the reasons for locating its sale in drug stores). The idea of banning dangerous things extends to books, pornography, and even the bomb. Unfortunately, while "banned in Boston" is an historically recurrent rallying cry, banning the substance does not seem to do much good. Perhaps the one area of greatest success is in scheduled drugs, but even there abuses abound.*

Controlling the user, a more internal mode of control, seems to have a greater degree of success. For example, in driving, the logical conclusion that the citizenry must learn how to drive resulted in a straightforward program of driver education which is virtually uncontested throughout the country. But classes in "how to drink" would be frowned upon as formal course offerings (some think that important components of higher education comprise exactly such an informal course!) and certainly courses in how to have effective sexual relations would be the subject of controversy. Current sex education classes are almost always under some kind of "concerned" review.

Hence, the definition of the area, the ideas surrounding it, make various kinds of interventions possible while foreclosing others. Driving classes are permissable; drinking classes are not. The residual concern that any kind of instruction would, in one way or another, increase the level of permission for actions seeking to be controlled is always present.

---

*   Sometimes abuses come in odd forms. In the case of older people and other users of many prescription drugs, the control works well drug by drug, but the interaction effects and attendent to drug combinations becomes the problem.

The alternate formulation sees alcoholism as the central problem to be defined, and so defines alcohol in a negative way. Like the cobalt bomb, the beverage has no redeeming social virtue and because of its totally problematic aspect, it must be severely controlled or banned.

The definition of the problem, then, at least within certain limits, is also a mechanism of permission and control. Some definitions are more permissive and open, others pave the way to greater control. Language is not neutral.

Rationality Versus Non-rationality (or Fault Versus No-fault)

Closely related to the intellectual definition of the problem is the definition of the causes of the alcohol problems. In particular, there is a conflict between rational causality on the one hand, versus irrational causality on the other. The first, of course, can be controlled. Things which have rational causes can be the "fault" of someone, who can then be punished. This predominant definition has varied over the years. The "enemy" drinker suggests and uses rationality causality. The "sick" drinker focuses upon uncontrollable aspects. The "responsible" drinker returns to rationality once again.

There is good reason to think about the functions these definitions serve for the definers. For example, ill-treatment (or non-helpful treatment) of minorities is consistent with, surprisingly enough, some American beliefs and values (Tropman, 1976). Beliefs in "equality of opportunity" do little for victims of discrimination. Attitudes toward the poor are important in this respect, too. In looking at the image of the poor (historcally it could have been called "the image of the alcoholic"), the attitudes and beliefs about the poor are seen as central to the social/psychological integrity of the non-poor person. Also important is the element of personal control, and the attribution of fault to the poor. People's attributions are seen as central, intellectual, and social/psychological underpinnings to their own sense of control of their environment. If the poor are at fault, then they are "deserving" of their fate (Tropman, 1976). The deservingness of poor people's fate is important, not to the poor person, but to the non-poor person because the non-poor person can use this assumption to also assume he deserves his higher, more well-off status.* The hypothesis is quite similar to the one developed by Walster, et al. (1978). They were concerned with the process of "attribution," or how people assign blame. In reviewing the most recent material on attribution, Wortman (1976) points to the research Walster did on assignment of blame in an auto accident scenario. She quotes as follows:

> As the magnitude of the misfortune increases ... it becomes more and more unpleasant to acknowledge that 'this is the kind of a thing that could happen to anyone.' ... If a serious accident is seen as the consequence of an unpredictable set of circumstances beyond anyone's control or anticipation, a person is forced to concede the catastrophe could happen to him.

---

* This issue is complex. Two assumptions are required: deservedness, which is a content assumption, and a structural assumption, viz., that the flow of fault and responsibility is symmetrical. Hence, it is not necessarily the same thing to assume that if the poor person deserves his fate the non-poor person deserves his fate also. In fact, charity is partly based upon the idea that, while the non-poor person deserves his fate, the poor person does not deserve his. This norm or belief may hold up to a point, but the overall attitude of distributive justice with respect to the stratification system is what is more usual. One would like to know under what conditions distributively just or unjust beliefs are held, and to what degree. (See Alves and Rossi, 1978).

> If, however, he decides that the event was a predictable, controllable one, if he decides that <u>someone</u> was responsible for the unpleasant event, he should feel somewhat more able to avert such a disaster (Wortman, 1976, p. 24).

A similar phenomenon might operate in alcohol attitudes. The harsher the attitude, the more controlling the belief system, and the more concern the holder of the attitude may have about personal control with respect to himself and his life space. This hypothesis could extend Gusfield's notion of status politics and temperance. Temperance, he argues, came into being when the old line Protestants felt threatened by the new Catholic immigrants. Temperance movements and attempts to control drinking were handy ways to exercise control. Political actions which have the maintenance of a superior social/moral position of one group over another as their purpose are called "status politics." Here, the gain is one of deference and personal good-feeling, rather than money or some other valued good. Status politics can be generated by those experiencing status-diminishment, in an attempt to gain a more favored position. It can, as in this instance, be exercised by those who are status-advantaged in order to retain previous position. Alcohol was "selected" or "handy" as a vehicle through which to assert moral superiority.

If the two-level hypothesis is correct, and the issue of alcohol actually is threatening in and of itself (as well as in its representations and meanings beyond its properties <u>sui generis</u>), then people's images about alcohol may be in part an attempt to deal with issues of fault and control within their own personal and social enviornment. As Walster, et al. (1978) suggest, attribution might well be an attempt at intellectual control - at conceptual control - which enables one to assert that the situation can be managed.

Over history the rationalists and the irrationalists - the fault finders and the fault freers - have battled back and forth over who would have intellectual and conceptual sway within the alcohol field. One needs to understand these battles in even larger terms than alcohol, and to view these as battles between permission and control in the society itself.

Internal Versus External Control

Given the importance of "control" in the attribution framework, it is important to consider the element of locus of control, or where control occurs. This distinction is one which has been developed in detail by Rotter (1966), but one can see it emerge throughout the history of attitudes and actions around alcohol. On the one hand, there are those who think the locus of control is himself or herself (and see such control over a range of elements in the life space); on the other hand, there are those who see control as primarily external (and see little they can do to influence events which affect their life space). This is related to the control of person/control of substance point mentioned a bit ago. There, the reference was the person versus an external element too. However, in that perspective, the focus was upon intervention, and which target would be the most sensible one and offer the greatest leverage. It was essentially a policy perspective. Here the perspective is social/psychological in nature, and focuses upon where the individual, himself or herself, sees the major center of control for life's events located, within or outside himself or herself.*

---

*   There are at least two aspects to consider here - what the person perceives is the beginning. What may actually be true is something else again. A person may think he is the locus of control, and perceives he has influence, but he may actually not have it. Social designations and preferences may be important as well. Social in this context means the "lore" in any society about fate, luck, chance, influence, etc.

Consistent with suggestions made throughout this monograph, it would be appropriate to expand the locus of control notion to a locus of permission/locus of control idea. There are two dimensions which are important, not just one. They can be internal or external - that is, permission can have internal or external components, and control can have internal or external components. They are seen in the following illustration:

Figure 4
Internal and External
Locus of Permission and Control

                Internal 3   External 4

Permission

Internal 1

External 2

There can, of course, be conflicts between any two orientations - six types of conflicts are yielded which might be useful to consider in more detail (1,2; 3,4; 1,3; 2,3; 1,4; 2,4). Two sets of these conflicts are within the vector (1,2;3,4); four are between permission and control dimensions. While it is too complex to consider here, it may be the specific nature of the conflict, rather than the fact of conflict itself, which makes an important difference in alcohol patterns in societies of the world, and in American society over time.

This suggestion expands the argument with those who suspect gap theories, which use conflict *sui generis* (as opposed, say, to tranquility) as a basis for explaining anything. There is probably no period without conflict (ambivalence). However, rather than its presence, it is its nature which is of interest.*

The dichotomy yields a fourfold table, as displayed in Figure 5. The figure has some interesting properties. In the uppper left cell (A) internal permission and internal control are harmonious. This type of society is typified by inner direction (to use Riesman, Glazer and Denney's (1961) term).**

The inner/inner cell is also the cell in which the primary group is extremely important, and primary controls, which flow from this group, are the most

---

*   "Gap" theories seek to identify a "space" between two variables as a generative force for action. For example, in cognitive dissonance there is a gap between what a person knows and experiences, leading to a "dissonant" state. In opportunity theory (the Cloward-Ohlin opportunity theory of delinquency) there is a gap between the culturally approved goals and culturally provided means (see Merton, 1957). There is no question these and other gaps exist. The issue is how they work, how people perceive them, and what people do about them. The permission/control idea is somewhat different. It suggests there are two relatively balanced forces which contend against the other.

** Reisman, et al. (1961), had three forms of direction - (1) from the past (tradition), (2) from inside oneself (inner), and (3) from others (other). "Inner" and "other" may well be similar to internal and external. These may be "pure" types, where both permission and control come from external or internal sources. Riesman, et al., also spoke of an "other" directed society. From this perspective, that could be a "mixed" direction, where permission was internal or external or control was internal or external. What those authors did not consider was the possibility of competing sources of permission *and* control leading to a somewhat more elaborated system than they suggested.

prevalent. Guilt is a primary mechanism relating to the internal permission/control balance, and within the individual is a way of not letting self-permission get out of hand.*

Figure 5
Social Patterns in Loci of Permission/Control

Permission   Control

	Internal	External
	Puritan Society (A)	Protestant Society (C)
Internal	Jewish Society Mormon Society American Society Repentent Drinker Guilt Orientation Inner Direction	Revival Society "Born Again" Society Female Society Enemy Drinker Other Direction
External	Roaring Twenties Society (B) Other Direction Sick Drinker	Catholic Society (D) Southern Society Male Society Japanese Society Responsible Drinker Tradition Direction Shame Orientation

* Since permission and control are two separate dimensions in this analysis, there is some need to comment upon their relationship to each other, viz., when does permission override control and control limit permissions? When they are both located within the individual, there is a need to prevent the individual from becoming too controlled (the authoritarian personality) or too permissive (the "bleeding heart"). Thus, guilt is a mechanism of control, which acts internally to limit permissions. We do not have a name for, and in this society have not paid much attention to, a mechanism analagous to guilt which limits control. Narcissism might be one candidate.

"Following" (if one uses an historical perspective) the inner/inner cell are two transition periods - inner/other and other/inner - which, finally, "lead" to the other/other cell. This is typified by both permission and control being located outside the individual.*

If cell A represents primary interaction, in which the locus of control and permission is located principally in the individual and in his surrounding primary group, then the inner/other and other/inner phases are secondary, or are communal controls, where the focus is on the individual interacting with his communal associates. The individual is still highly important here, as a key locus of either permission or control.**

Cell D, external/external, represents a situation where both important controls and important permissions are external to the individual. In its extreme form, it might be a totalitarian regime, but there are other manifestations of it as well. In its early phase, behaviorism represented an extreme form of external control/permission, although other developments in self-reinforcing activity suggest a return to balance (Karpfl and Vargas, 1977). In its most extreme form, social Darwinism (Tax and Krucoff, 1964) suggested the individual was simply a pawn in the larger game of life-forces acting out an inexorable course. From an

* Care should be taken not to regard the sequence of letters as "progress" of any sort. Rather, they represent different episodes in the life of society, and a society (as a whole) may well move from one to another and "back" again. Subsocieties within an overall society, as is suggested in the figure, may well be modally identified or characterized by location in one cell, but even this assignment should be viewed as hueristic.

** This approach suggests primary, secondary, and (in a moment) tertiary levels of permission/control, and is consistent with the "triple community" analysis developed earlier, in which secondary associations are seen as mainly "communal" in nature (see Tropman and Erlich, 1979).

entirely different perspective, Marxism can be seen in this light as well - alienation of the individual becoming, in this scheme, separation of the individual from possession of either permission or control responsibilities.*

The 1970s and '80s in America is a period in which an external/external ethic is popular and dominant. The external permission phase extended up into the '60s, and from the substance abuse point of view expanded from alcohol into many other kinds of drugs and substances. At that time it appeared to many Americans that things were "out of control" - colleges, cities, sexual behavior. Society is now in a phase of developing more external controls, strengthening internal ones, and withdrawing permissions, although the course is an uneven one. The Michigan Legislature, for example, lowered the penalties on "pot" and raised the drinking age within the same month. However, the increased attention to alcohol problems, the increased sensitivity to alcohol-related vehicular fatalities, and the increasing number of campaigns to involve others (other than the self) in alcohol control are illustrative of the trend. For example, a poster suggests family influence by depicting a man in a chair with several cans of beer around him

---

* Marxism - and devaluation of individual control under Marxism - could be seen as a having some similarities to a secular analogue to predestination, which similarly removed permission and control of celestial matters and the direction of one's soul from the individual. But Marxism is more clearcut about the structure of the situation (external) determining what happens to the individual in terms of permissions and controls over behavior. Puritanism is more ambivalent - because of the Predestination ethic. The fact that things are not always what they seem is well illustrated here. While the ethic of predestination is a good example of an external/external orientation, the fact that one could <u>indicate</u> his or her status through worldly success transformed the <u>effect</u> of the ethic (as opposed to the ethic itself) into a highly inner/inner directed form.

watching tv, and a young person about 3-4 years old, obviously his son, sitting watching him. The caption reads something like, "Got the feeling you are being watched?"

It is this last period which Meyerson refers to as "Enlightened Hedonism" or, in our terms, the "responsible drinker." There is an interest in substances - not just alcohol, but other drugs of a medical and non-medical variety as well - and a disposition on the part of society to be permissive, as long as certain parameters of control are obtained. When those boundaries are crossed, then society will react, as it is beginning to, by increasing external and internal controls.

As noted, the use of the family strengthens internal controls. The use of legislative action to change drinking ages, to seek to regulate and control the use of alcohol, represents external controls. Of course both can be going on simultaneously, and as the next phase we can probably anticipate moving back into an inner permission/inner control period.

This last type of permission and control - the external/external group - is "tertiary controls," or controls which affect an individual, not because of interaction with others or because they have been implanted into his self-concept, but because he or she is a member of a collectivity and is entitled and required, by virtue of that membership. This position is consistent with Gronjberg's analysis (1977) of the extension of welfare benefits in the 1960s.*

---

*   Note here Lipset's distinction between achievement orientation and egalitarian orientation (1963), which he sees as being so important in American history. From one point of view (Tropman and Gordon, 1978), achievement orientation is similar to inner permission/control, while egalitarian orientation is similar to external permission/control.

In sum, one can see a shift in locus of control balance over time between inner and other, internal and external loci and better permission and control. There is, of course, always conflict at each of these four junctures which makes them a juncture for societal friction and contest.

Conflicts within the cells could be called intra-dimensional conflicts; between them are inter-dimensional conflicts. A shift in their balance, whatever that balance is at any point in time, may be the "first domino" which triggers a cyclical adjustment. Thus, a shift from internal control to external control may set up a new phase (from cell A to cell B, for example) and initiate a change from internal to external permission, while at the same time setting up conditions for a return to internal control. If this process seems like one of constant adjustment and readjustment - of both intra system and inter system properties - it is. Perhaps driving is the best example. One can draw an absolutely parallel line down the middle of each lane, but no one drives like that. Rather, there is a dynamic interaction betwen car, driver, road, and weather, each of which vary independently and together. The boxes are simply a stroboscopic "freezing" of a dynamic process of continual adjustment and readjustment. In society, as in driving, there is no magic. Sometimes corrections work, sometimes they fail (often called "overcorrecting"), and sometimes additional mechanisms need to be introduced. Sometimes the introduction of corrective measures cause more problems than the original problem.

An additional point to emphasize is that all of these cells (and processes) occur all of the time. What we are referring to is not exclusively one as opposed to another, but rather dominance of one at a given moment in time. The others are somewhat more latent as one is manifest. No period is characterized by only one mode.

Furthermore, various sub-parts of the society at any given moment or during various periods of history may be more typical of one intersection than another. At great peril we have listed some groups (all called "societies") in the various cells to suggest some cultures and structures which might loosely "fit" this model. We hope that the reader views these nominations charitably, as suggestions rather than as definitions. We indicated that the society was composed of many forces: acting, interacting and reacting. This figure accounts for these forces by showing the range of different intersections which can occur at any given point in time, among sub-groups, regions or periods of history.

Mastery Versus Drift

Following the two level assumption, the contest of permission/control within American society is played out at the levels of society and person. One must always take care that both aspects of the issue are considered. Having discussed the cultural and social structure, it is appropriate to consider the person. There are two features of an individual's drinking patterns which need to be considered here: use and abuse.

Up till now, the orientation here has been to discuss permission and control _of_ drinking. Now, however, there needs to be consideration of permission and control _through_ drinking. It appears that people seek both permission and control through alcohol, and some of each may be a desired end state. While this "state" is at the level of the individual, certain social conditions may aggravate, or pacify conditions at the level of the individual person.*

---

*   Perhaps a good, non-alcohol example is the work of Harvy Brenner, Mental Health and the Economy (1973). He shows an inverse correlation between "good economic times" and admissions to state mental hospitals, controlling for many other possible relationships. Interestingly enough, this finding occurs for men more so than women. It suggests that psychological states have an important link with conditions of the social structure, on a patterned basis. There is no reason to think something similar would not be true for alcohol use and abuse.

As McClelland (1972) and his colleagues have suggested, one hypothesis is that people drink to achieve power or a sense of power. Using the framework developed here, it would be similar to think about a sense of mastery over events opposed to a sense of drifting with the tide of events (Lippmann, 1961). Of course the need for such control may vary with the historical periods and social structures. It may also vary with individual psychological states, and with what types of releases are available given the person and the relevant environments.

But at the individual level the control needs to be seen within the context of permission. It's "ok" to do certain things, to express certain feelings, to become "drunk."* It is important to see both power and permission in the equation. Different people (on a psychological level) and different people in different groups (on a social-psychological level) may have different needs for permission and control.**

What might some of these "needs" be? Rorabaugh (1979) suggests that anxiety might be a factor. In a long chapter in his book, The Alcoholic Republic, called "The Anxieties of Their Condition," he talks about a number of anxieties, some of a structural sort, which afflicted the people of the American republic during the early 19th century. Among the anxiety-provoking factors mentioned are the poor condition of farm laborers (as opposed to the prosperous condition of farmers), the collapse of the guilds, and anxieties of class and rank

*   To a degree, this appears to be a dominant motive within Japanese society. See the discussion of businessmen's drinking in Seward (1972).

** To some extent, permission may be an aspect of power, and vice versa. The inter-relationships and possible connections between these two concepts are too complex to explore here. But if power were a way to legitimate or provide permission, then a rich literature could be brought to bear. Whatever else it may be, power is permission to do things.

(pp. 133-134). He also talks about the anxieties implicit in the rootlessness of lumbermen, canal diggers, and the like, and the alienation of certain groups, especially the Irish.

He defines anxiety as the ratio between level of aspiration and level of achievement orientation.* In a striking section, developed almost in passing, he relates different levels of aspiration/achievement to different types of need for anxiety release, arguing that "If Horton's theory that drinking allays anxiety is correct, then we would expect the most potent alcoholic beverages to be used to cope with the greatest anxieties" (Rorabaugh, 1979, p. 174). It is an arresting hypothesis (literally, in some cases). On a psychological level, Rorabaugh "explains" the different types of beverages people may drink by the aspiration/achievement orientation ratio. While he himself does not put it in a fourfold table, it is easy to do and is displayed in Figure 6.

High anxiety occurs in persons with high aspirations but low achievement orientation, so that the "gap" (implicitly) between what they want and what they can get is great. The people with high aspirations but whose achievement orientation gives them some sense of accomplishment over the situation are more likely to be wine drinkers. The low/low group are likely to be beer drinkers, and those who have an achievement surplus are

---

* There is a certain similarity here too to the work of Merton (1958) on means and ends. Implicitly, anxiety would occur when the ratio is less than 1 or greater than 1. The anxieties may differ, of course, when one feels less success than one wants, or has too much success. Men and women may differ here as well (Gilligan, 1982). Rorabaugh focuses upon the situation in which the ratio is less than 1. He does not consider "fear of success" or the possibility of "fear from success" when the ratio is greater than 1.

likely to be abstainers.* If one refers back to Figure 1, certain similarities emerge between it and Figure 4. One could regard aspirations as a personal equivalent to permission, and achievement orientation as a personal equivalent to control.

Figure 6
Type of Alcoholic Beverage Consumed By Relationship Between Aspirations and Achievement Orientation
(after Rorabaugh)

		Achievement	
		Low	High
Aspirations	Low	Beer 1	Abstain 4
	High	Liquor 3	Wine 2

(1) = moderate anxiety (3) = high anxiety
(2) = moderate anxiety (4) = low anxiety

* See Rorabaugh (1979), p. 174. His use seems consistent with Atkinson's definition, viz., "motivation to achieve is instigated when an individual knows he is responsible for the outcome of some venture, when he anticipates explicit knowledge of results that will define his success or failure, and when there is some degree of risk, i.e., some uncertainty about the outcome of his effort" (Atkinson, 1968, Vol. 1, p. 27). Some question must be raised about "abstainers." It seems plausible that anxiety of a sort Rorabaugh did not anticipate could be present in those who had low(er) aspirations and high(er) achievements. But this point must await further explanation in more detail.

Rorabaugh himself comments as follows:

> Thus a person's choice of alcoholic beverage can be related to the level of his anxieties, and, by inference, to the level of motivation for achievement and the level of aspiration. Among high aspirers the higly motivated have the ability to strive towards goals, suffer some anxiety from the attempt, and drink wine; those with low motivations have less confidence in their ability to reach targets, suffer great anxiety, and drink whiskey. Among low aspirers the highly motivated find it easy to gain minimal expectations, are free of anxiety, and abstain; the lower motivated find it difficult to attempt to reach even lower gaols, suffer some anxiety, and drink beer (Rorabaugh, 1979, pp. 174-175).

If one were to make the connection between the aspiration/achievement focus and the one suggested here, then the drinking styles suggested by Rorabaugh would fit into the cells of Figure 3. Low permission/low control societies would be the beer/cider group; high permission/high control societies would be the wine group - previously called the "responsible drinker." Low permission/high control societies would be the abstaining group, those which were called the "sick" drinker period (after Gusfield). Finally, societies with high permission/low control would be the liquor groups, the "enemy" drinker. (By the way, these "societies" could also be time periods, as suggested in Figure 1.) The fit is far from perfect, but it is sufficiently close enough to be interesting. Achievement motivation represents an interesting choice. There is a competitive aspect in the definition of achievement which involves uncertainty in contests with others. Atkinson writes, "The goal of achievement-oriented activity is to succeed, to perform well in relationship to a standard of excellence or in comparison with others who are competitors" (Atkinson 1968, Vol. 1, p. 27).

Atkinson comments further on "achievement imagery in fantasy" which sometimes involves being blocked. This suggestion immediately calls to mind Rorabaugh's discussion of the fantasies involved in cases of alcoholic delerium tremens. Drawing upon accounts of the period, Rorabaugh reports that the fantasy involved people believing that they were pursued, either by people or animals:

> Such a paranoid view could easily develop in a culture that rejected paternalism and stressed autonomy and where great competitiveness was encouraged and lauded. At a time when American values stressed the virtue of competition it is not surprising that delirious drinkers who felt endangered by rivals imagined themselves to be threatened by snakes, mice or rats as well as by travelling companions or landlords" (Rorabaugh, 1979, p. 172).

What is still unclear, perhaps, is the " . . . agreement that anxiety - as a mediating, experiential phenomenon - is related to the perception of impending threat . . . although there may be differences of opinion on the nature of this threat" (Mandler, 1968, Vol. 1 p. 363) The existentialists argue that there is no way of coping with ". . . the anxiety that goes with possibility and freedom." (Mandler, 1968, Vol. 1, p. 364, emphasis added) Possiblility and freedom sound a lot like permission, and high permission situations may generate a psychological predisposition to drink, as well as the feeling that it is "OK" to do so. Rorabaugh comments, almost as if he were following Mandler right along:

> It was guilt that made the drinker's hallucination a hellish world in which American ideals were

> inverted: thus did the striving for autonomy become a fear of others, the belief in equality a fear that others were superior - like a giant rat. Even the desire to exploit the material world became an impotent rage in which men felt themselves to be manipulated by the devil. These guilt-laden and paranoiac deliriums may reveal underlying fears that gripped Americans. (Rorabaugh, 1979, p. 173)

There is a question, though, about whose anxieties need to be relieved, and in what way - how "relief" is to be administered. If the line of analysis here has merit, then two sorts of motivations are needed, and drinking may result not from a single but from a dual causal framework. Certainly drinking creates permission, but in doing so it may also create more anxiety, resulting explicitly from that greater permission. That is, unless one drinks in a well defined situation, with well defined controls which accompany these greater permissions. It is perhaps to structure the greater permissions which come from drinking as well as their attendant anxieties that make the drinking setting so important.

It may also be that one can interpret the drinking patterns of men and women in a related way. Men are involved in situations of great control, where feelings need to be masked or shuttered. Thus they are in greater need of assistance in generating increased permissions. Men may also experience greater permissions than women to begin with, but in spite of the greater control may feel there is not enough control to be "successful." Others - competitors - are always ready to close in. Men may be in the situation, then, of greater permissions and insufficient control, but "insufficient" for what? They are insufficient to meet the demands placed upon them, to cope with the uncertainties and problems of their responsibilities.

In a very important sense, alcohol may be seen as a

weapon to gain greater control over the environment. A story in Yankee magazine about a drinking man illustrates this point nicely concerning alcohol's dual purpose. It is a friend. The protagonist says:

> Alcohol has always been a friend I could count on, unlike most of my other friends. Life in the business world is no picnic, and just when you need someone is the time he generally picks to disappear (Meinke, 1979, pp. 114-115).

How is alcohol a friend? In this case, it relieves his tension:

> . . . and martini and the liver pate and stuffed mushrooms and shrimp cocktail all go to the back of your neck and untie that knot that seemed permanent until this very moment and you smile thankfully. . . (Meinke, 1979, pp. 114-115).)

But alcohol has another dimension as well. It is a weapon which one uses in the very competition itself.

> Of course most men nowadays are proud of their capacities; it is one of the New Frontiers. The action today is not in the Wild West, but in the Business Lunch, and instead of shoot-outs, we have drinkouts: may the best man win. It's no accident that those short lethal drinks are called shots, that we get bombed and blasted; even the later stoned and paralyzed imply a violent metaphor. It works also the other way: Molotov Cocktails (Meinke, 1979, p. 114, emphasis in original.)

Therefore, alcohol is here, as everywhere else, a

73

two-edged sword. It is an attempt to control (or attack others who themselves control) goods and services, benefits and perequisites, which the individual competitior wants. Alcohol thus not only makes men feel powerful, it can actually be used to make them powerful. It can be used for pleasure, or for competition.

There may be, therefore, a complex combination of reasons for choosing a powerful drink in a high anxiety situation - one may need the most potent weapon one can find, to aid himself, or to use to attack others.

This is the problem with the anxiety hypothesis, then. While alcohol relieves anxiety, it may raise it as well. Indeed, it may be at this point that the cycle of alcohol abuse begins. For yet unknown reasons, anxiety release and anxiety generation operate in a reinforcing tandem when high permissions generate a sense of high control of others, which in turn generate additional anxieties, requiring more control, and so on. Wherever there is a situation of balance, as there is supposed to be in the permission/control framework, there can be certain situations in which the brake sends one into a skid, and attempts to reduce the anxiety generated through alcohol may actually only increase it, at least for men.

Women, on the other hand, may be low on permission and also low on control. Thus, the level of anxiety generated there is less, and they may affect less drinking and milder beverages. As women move into the work force and are exposed to the same expectations as men - by themselves and others - they may experience an increased permission/control gap which may, in turn, generate patterns similar to men. With individuals with low/low tendencies, the norms may eventually change, closing the permission/control gap overall.

Here is perhaps the point at which social condition and pyschological condition touch. After all, anxieties are predicated on not only what the individual can do, but on what society provides for that individual, and on the perceptions that individual has of the nature of the society and the expectations placed thereon. In each case, there is ample room for variance and change.

Perhaps nowhere more than in America, individuals seek to be masters of their own fate. Permission is high for them to do this, and control is low to moderate. If one thinks about permissions as ends and controls as means, then there is a means-end chain in which many of the people have similar ends but radically different means. For some, this means-ends gap (which is the essence of what Rorabaugh was talking about) may be the pressing problem which generates a need for "powerful" drink.

If mastery is to be achieved and drift avoided, however, there are some other reasons why strong drink might be preferable, too. For one thing, in American society time is essential. Whatever happens must happen "fast." As Rorabaugh points out, we do not seek to savor food, it is instrumental. A similar point might be made about relationships - once they have served their "purpose," they are discarded.* We are not a savoring society. Similarly (or because of it) this society has much geographic mobility. While Rorabaugh points to the "anxieties of class," referring to social and occupational mobility, the actual geographic mobility gets less attention. We are always going somewhere, and fast. Each of these traits could certainly be associated with a preference for strong drink, and strong drink exclusively. Why exclusively? Because Rorabaugh's hypothesis, interesting as it is, leaves aside the troubling point that the same level inebriation can be achieved by taking more of a weaker drink. Without some way to account for why that alternative is not attractive, his theory is incomplete.

Similarly, the mobile society further supports this line of thinking. For people physically on the move, something which can be carried in a small space but which has high power is to be valued; something which does not need controlled temperatures or which does

---

*   Relationships appear to have different meanings for men and women. See Gilligan (1982).

not need to be chilled is also valuable. The mobile society had limited space to carry beer and wine. Whiskey is the pocket calculator of the alcohol trade - high production in a small space.

Conclusion

The variables discussed in this chapter are all important to the permission/control complex. Each has an important association with alcohol; each has broader implications with respect to the permission/control issue in general. The movement through history, suggested in the previous chapter, may be a false movement. The issues may always be present, but in different packages and combinations at different points in time. Each perspective - the historical and the ahistorical - provided part of a view on the issues of drinking in American society.

CHAPTER SIX

PERMISSION AND CONTROL
IN A COMMUNAL SOCIETY

Given the theme of this volume, one might be inclined to consider permission/control an individual problem. Or it might seem a group/gender problem, where certain group memberships permit or control drinking (Irish versus Jews, for example) or where gender-related differences come to the fore in a prominent way. And certainly these variables <u>are</u> important.

But these variables exist in a societal context, and this context needs a final examination, especially because the reinterpretation of the contextual structure called American society sheds light on the problems of permission and the conundrums of control.

The Communal Society

Typically, American society is thought of as an individualistic society, one in which the individual is lionized and things communal and common are devalued. Communities and committees are but two examples of the negative view that collective efforts have. Yet it seems this public view is like many public ideas: only part of the story. A more correct perception might be be one which sees American society as between the "independent model" and the "interdependent" one. Perhaps a phrase like "uncertain interdependence" would hit the right note. Or one might call it the communal society.

The communal society is less individualistic than many may have assumed. Much depends upon the group

- and perhaps the wagon train is the perfect symbol of the country's character. There are individual wagons, each with its individual occupants, "pulling its own weight."

But the very train itself is what makes progress possible. One cannot pull one wagon into a circle! The wagon train embodies the collectivism and individualism in the society itself, and the uneasy tension between them. It represents communal society, a society in which the individual is prominent but the group close behind. The fact that our society promotes the individual does not mean that the group drops from sight. On the contrary, the group is omnipresent, helping us reach our goals, and providing assistance in many ways. We are highly dependent upon the group for much of the structure which makes our individual achievement possible. Yet the key problematic point is that our ideology denies rather than recognizes the interdependency. We are all dependent upon the other wagons in the train, and we don't like it. Why not? The answer may lie in the very issues which are so prominent in understanding drinking - power and control. Interdependency means a loss of control and direction, a sense that one must wait upon others to get permission (and help) to go ahead. But what is so bad about this? Nothing except that the individual, in this heavily Protestant society, is responsible for himself. Thus, myth varies with reality, and the myth of individualism is located within a context of dependency and interdependency. To a degree the individual believes that he is captain of his own body and soul.

Yet for him to get where he wants to, he must depend upon the first mate, <u>whom he does not control</u>.

Rorabaugh puts it this way:

> The protestant belief that man must act as his own agent to save himself, the stress on attaining educational skills in order to read and understand the Bible, and the turning of one's guilt about one's

> inadequacies into a driving mechanism to achieve both success and visible proof of one's worthiness are all conducive to striving for goals (Rorabaugh, 1979, p. 181).*

He notes further the problems that this kind of orientation creates:

> One problem, I think is that trying to live up to the ideal of the independent man was a burden too heavy for many people to carry (Rorabaugh, 1979, p. 172).

Perhaps this difficulty is seen in the metaphor of the Lone Ranger. Of course, he was not "alone." He had an Indian with him to help and assist him, who did his bidding. An Indian is an interesting choice here, because he is almost a non-person in terms of American regard. But time after time that "non-person" was crucially important to the Lone Ranger. Consider the situation of the Lone Ranger (each of us, in a way) not in "control" of his aide (society in the largest sense; our husband, wife, children, boss, etc., in the smaller), then we are left vulnerable, which generates both anxiety (and guilt) and a need for control. Each is related to alcohol use.

---

* This statement captures the essence of the "Protestant Ethic" motivation that Weber (1956) developed. I need to add only one caveat. It was not so much guilt which was the driving motivational force in that motivational scheme, but uncertainty about whether or not one was saved (or, in more secular terms, "ok"). That uncertainty became the dynamo behind the constant acquisitive drive of the "acquisitive society." And while it was true to a degree that man needed to act on his own, it was uncertain whether this action could save him; it might just reveal whether or not he had passed the test.

The need for control has already been considered. Now it can be seen in a somewhat broader context. What is the "it" that we need to control? First, "it" is ourselves - because we are dependent upon significant others in the society, and our ideology does not allow that to be acceptable. Alcohol enhances (if falsely) the sense of control. But it is also a mode of controlling others. Alcohol is a weapon, perhaps as potent as the gun itself. It is used to control others, by besting them in "drinking duels." It is this latent dual aspect which, in drinking, so often erupts into physical violence - perhaps not because alcohol "permits true feelings" to come out, but because drinking itself is an aggressive act.

It may be that drinking patterns reveal the central threats in the society itself. Drinking with "buddies" may mean, for men, that other men are the central threat, the ones with whom contests need to be established, and who need to be bested. Solo bouts may reflect that the element is control of the person himself, but it is the person himself who needs to reestablish power over himself. Drinking in the family may reveal that the family (man, wife and children) is the source of most problems of control, both for the individual and for society.

Rorabaugh points to a gap - a ratio - between aspiration and achievement. Here we have a tension between self-reliance and dependency. It is not simply to say that the more dependency exists, the more one seeks control; there is also the extent to which one is expected to be independent, and the extent to which one controls the means through which independence can be achieved, and on which one will be judged.

There may be important differences in gender here which could be woven into the overall picture of drinking differences. Women may have less (or modest) control over a range of events in their life than men, but they may have some control <u>over the events on which they will be judged</u>. Indeed, this type or realm of control may be among the most important. Perhaps one does not need control over everything - there may be a few crucial elements where control is important.

Others would be nice, but not essential. Men, on the other hand, may be in a situation where they do not control as many of the elements over which they will be judged, and therefore have a greater need for more control.

A second element of the communal society concept may effect the situation here - uncertainty. Roger Hilsman talks about Professor Joseph Brown of Princeton, who designed a sort of geodesic dome with elastic nylon lines stretched between and among the poles. It was a playground toy.

> He built a spider web of this special rope in the shape of a pyramid, and then tightened the strands until each was in vibrating tension with every other. The results were dramatic: if an impish child in a crowd of climbers plucked a strand on one side of the pyramid, some startled innocent on the other would find himself flung violently in several directions at once. The taut nylon web was so intricately interwoven that there was no sure way of telling who had been the original culprit, so the game of retaliation and counter-retaliation usually led to what can be described as complex pandemonium. . . . Professor Brown's greatest pride (was in) . . . the educational contribution. 'The children,' he said, 'learn two profound truths about life. The first is that there are so-and-so's in the world. The second, and more important, is that it's not easy to be sure just who they are' (Hillsman, 1976, p. 22).

Brown mentions an apt metaphor for the communal society. We are highly dependent upon people, many of whom we may not know. The problems of control are thus generalized (making the concept of social control, mentioned in the opening pages, crucial) and one may never be sure exactly whom one needs to control.

This situation may represent a form of anxiety. The uncertainty is twofold - first, what might happen; and second, who might be responsible. It seems reasonable to argue that men and women (as well as other collectivities) differ in the amount and nature of the uncertainty which affects them in their daily lives. But what of guilt? Guilt can be thought of as the psychological residue of undeserved gain. One does not feel guilty when one feels a particular reward has been earned, or when one has "paid his due." However, the communal society is also the guilty society - because one can never be fully self-reliant. Everyone knows that some of any individual's achievements are due to the work of others, however unacknowledged that work may be. The key is that the individual knows it, too.* This guilty knowledge places one in a position of debtor to the society itself - we know we "owe," yet the terms and conditions are unspecified. Two possible bad results are latent here, each of which drives up anxiety and reinforces the need for control.

The first bad result is that "others" may find out that we do not deserve what we have (and it may be taken from us). The social and personal meaning of those gains is thus tarnished, much as if someone found out that a Ph.D. dissertation had been forged. The intellectual competence of that dissertation is undercut by the discovery and makes that achievement hollow. Therefore, much energy must go into the preservation of the myth of individualism - which is the myth of control - against discovery. Under current ethos, that discovery will shatter the individual's sense of self-respect, however erroneously based that sense might be.

* It seems that women recognize these interdependent interconnections more than men, and are committed to their importance and maintenance (Gilligan, 1982).

But let us assume that the indivdual knows that he or she is interdependent with others for some of his or her achievements. He may feel the need to pay back or to contribute to the common weal that has treated him so well. The philanthropic impulse is substantial in this country, and is not confined to the robber barons, who tried belatedly to look like Robin Hood. (Their only problem was that they stole from the poor and gave to the rich!) In 1983, the budget of the nonprofit sector was $200 billion, including voluntary contributions (Tropman and Tropman, forthcoming). Philanthropy is the example, not the issue. The communal society involves everyone in a complex network of obligation all the more powerful because the obligations are unacknowledged and often uncertain. The anxiety stems from no clear way of repayment - one needs to wait for the phone to ring, and a requesting voice tells what the payment, for now, will be. Thus, the uncertainty is dual - uncertainty about who may be a threat or harm (over whom one may need control) as well as uncertainty about what one might owe (the requests that the society, the other members of the wagon train, might make). Both types of uncertainty have the need for greater control in common.

Conclusion

Societies are composed of conflicting values. The view expressed here is that these conflicting values come in pairs or sets, and are "bonded" together such that each acts as a restraint/constraint on the other. One example of such a set is the need of society for both permission and control. This values pair was used to look at alcohol attitudes and practices in historical and contemporary America.

Different points on the permission/control balance help us achieve perspective on a particular period of history's view of alcohol, or among or between various groups. Tensions generated by the achievement of one particular point on the balance scale become generative of change and movement toward another point (Parsons, 1951).

American society, then, is an uncertain trumpet, a call with competing and conflicting directions. Perhaps all societies are like this in some respects. That assessment must wait upon detailed comparative analysis of various value systems. But certainly for the United States, the promise of progress was accompanied by much uncertainty and anxiety, and the individual ethos of the society put a heavy burden upon the individual person to allay those anxieties and set aside those uncertainties. Perhaps their presence gives Americans a greater need for control than is present in other societies. If the cultural context is contradictory and both hopeful and perilous, then the individual may be left without much guidance about what is the approved and appropriate way to go. Freedom creates a concomitant need for control. Perhaps it is this need, the very openness of society itself, that stimulates drinking, and dictates, to a degree at least, the kind of drink as well.

The purpose of this volume has been to use the idea of cultural conflict stemming from dual values to illuminate the area of alcohol history. That history was seen as a contest between permission to drink and control of drinking. Alcohol actions were a useful device for this purpose because they are surrounded, sui generis, with issues of control. Certainly drinking generates increased permissions in the drinking setting, permissions enhanced by the permission-positive culture of the setting itself, and these enhancements may require increased controls (drink limits in some cases, bouncers in others). However, alcohol seems to be associated as well with an increased sense of personal control (almost always a false sense, to be sure), and that combination of permission and control extensions must give it its world wide appeal. Rorabaugh captures these twin themes.

> Alcohol, on the other hand [ed. note: as opposed to opium] enables a man to strive harder by decreasing inhibitions. Liquor is in this way more closely associated with the unleashing of aggression (Rorabaugh, 1979, p. 178).

As both indicator and an instance, then, alcohol is at the nexus of the contest over permission and control in American society. What seems important from this analysis is the perspective of dynamic development and counterbalancing commitment. Whatever policy/practice package is in place at the moment is, in itself [through tension with competing values and the disappointment mentioned by Hirshman (1982)] generative of change forces. However, the change is not something totally different, totally new. Rather the change is another aspect of our commitments which have been ignored for a while and are not resurfacing. In a very real sense, the more things change the more they remain the same.

REFERENCES

Agee, James. *A Death in the Family.* New York: Bantam, 1971.

Alves, W. and Peter Rossi. "Who Should Get What." *American Journal of Sociology* 84, 3 (November 1978): 541-564.

Anderson, C. Arnold. "Social Order." In J. Gould and W. L. Kolb (Eds.), *A Dictionary of the Social Sciences.* New York: The Free Press, 1964.

Atkinson, J. "Achievement Motivation." In D. Sills, (Ed.). *International Encyclopedia of the Social Sciences.* New York: Macmillan and the Free Press, 1968.

Bacon, Selden D. "The Classic Temperance Movement of the U.S.A.: Impact Today on Attitudes, Action and Research." *British Journal of Addiction* 62, 1/2 (March 1967): 5-18.

Banfield, Edward C. and James Q. Wilson. *City Politics.* Cambridge: Harvard University Press, 1963.

Bell, Daniel. *The End of Ideology.* Glencoe, IL: The Free Press, 1960.

Benedict, Ruth. *The Chrysanthemum and the Sword.* New York: Mentor, 1946.

Billington, Ray H. *The Protestant Crusade.* New York: Macmillan, 1938.

Brenner, M. Harvey. *Mental Illness and The Economy.* Cambridge, MA: Harvard University Press, 1973.

Cahalan, Don and Ira H. Cisin. "Drinking Behavior and Drinking Problems in the United States." In Benjamin Kissin and Henri Begleiter (Eds.), *Social Aspects of Alcoholism,* New York: Plenum Press, 1976.

Caplan, P. and I. Hale-McCorquodale. Mother Blaming in Major Clinical Journals." *American Journal of Orthopsychiatry* 55, 3 (June 1985): 345-353.

City/County Databook. Washington: U.S. Government Printing Office, 1971.

Cohen, Wilbur. "Social Insurance." In J. Turner

(Ed.), Encyclopedia of Social Work, New York: National Association of Social Workers, 1977.

Cumming, Elaine. "Allocation of Care to the Mentally Ill, American Style." In M.M. Zald (Ed.), Organizing for Community Welfare, Chicago: Quadrangle, 1967.

Durkheim, Emile. The Division of Labor in Society. (Translated by George Simpson). Glencoe, IL: The Free Press, 1947.

Edelman, Murray. Political Language. New York: Academic Press, 1977.

Erickson, Kai. Everything in its Path. New York: Simon and Shuster, 1976.

Fischer, D.H. Growing Old in America. New York: Oxford, 1978.

Gilligan, Carol. In A Different Voice. Cambridge: Harvard University Press, 1982.

Globetti, G. "Approaches to the Control of Alcoholic Beverages in the United States." Journal of Drug Issues 3 (1973): 260-266.

Gouldner, Alvin W. "Cosmopolitans and Locals: An Analysis of Latent Social Roles - I." Administrative Science Quarterly (December 1957): 281-306.

Gouldner, Alvin W. "Cosmpolitans and Locals: An Analysis of Latent Social Roles - II." Administrative Science Quarterly (March 1958): 444-480.

Greer, Germaine. Sex and History. New York: Harper and Row, 1984.

Gronbjerg, Kirsten A. Mass Society and the Extension of Welfare, 1960-1970. Chicago: University of Chicago Press, 1977.

Gusfield, Joseph R. "Moral Passage: The Symbolic Process in Public Designnations of Deviance." Social Problems 15, 2 (Fall 1967): 175-188.

Gusfield, Joseph R. "The Problem of Generations in an Organizational Structure." Social Forces 35, 4 (May 1957): 323-330.

Gusfield, Joseph R. Symbolic Crusade: Status Politics and the American Temperance Movement. Urbana, Ill.: University of Illinois Press, 1963.

Hawley, Amos H. Human Ecology. New York: The Ronald Press, 1950.

Hilsman, R. "Policy Making is Politics." In J. Tropman, et al. (Eds.), Strategic Perspectives on Social

Policy. Elmsford, NY: Pergamon Press, 1976.

Hirshman, Albert O. Shifting Involvements. Princeton: Princeton University Press, 1982.

Hudson, W. American Protestantism. Chicago: The University of Chicago Press, 1961.

Janowitz, Morris. Social Control of the Welfare State. New York: Elsevier, 1976.

Jellinek, E.M. "The Symbolism of Drinking: A Culture-Historical Approach." In R.E. Popham and C.D. Yawney (Eds.), Journal of Studies on Alcohol 38, 5 (May 1977): 849-866.

Jellinek, E.M. "Recent Trends in Alcoholism and in Alcohol Consumption." Quarterly Journal of Studies on Alcohol 8, 1 (June 1947): 1-42.

Karpfl, Jorn E. and Ernest Vargas. Behaviorism and Ethics. Kalamazoo: Behaviordelia, 1977.

Kates, Don B. (Ed.). Firearms and Violence. Cambridge: Ballinger, 1984.

Kolb, William L. "Moral Order." In Julius Gould and William L. Kolb (Eds.), A Dictionary of Social Sciences, New York: The Free Press of Glencoe, 1964.

Krock, Arthur. Memoirs. New York: Funk and Wagnalls, 1968.

Lender, Mark. "Drunkenness as an Offense in Early New England: A Study of 'Puritan' Attitudes." Quarterly Journal of Alcohol Studies 34, 2 (1973): 353-366.

Lifton, Robert Jay, Shuichi Kato and Michael R. Reich. Six Lives, Six Deaths. New Haven, CT: Yale University Press, 1979.

Linsky, Arnold. "Theories of Behavior and the Image of the Alcoholic in Popular Magazines, 1900-1966." The Public Opinion Quarterly 34 (Winter, 1970-71): 573-581.

Lippmann, Walter. Drift and Mastery. Westport: Greenwood, 1961.

Lipset, Seymour M. The First New Nation. New York: Basic Books, 1963.

Lynd, Robert. Knowledge for What. Princeton: Princeton University Press, 1939.

Mandler, George. "Anxiety." In D. Sills (Ed.), International Encyclopedia of the Social Sciences, New York: Macmillan and the Free Press, 1968.

McClelland, D., et al. The Drinking Man. New

York: The Free Press, 1972.

Meinke, P. "'Conversation with a Pole.'" Yankee 43, 10 (October, 1979).

Merton, R. Social Theory and Social Structure. Glencoe, IL: The Free Press, 1957.

Merton, Robert. Social Theory and Social Structure, Revised Edition. Glencoe, IL: The Free Press, 1958.

Myerson, Abraham. "Alcohol: A Study of Social Ambivalence." Quarterly Journal of Studies on Alcohol 1, 1 (June 1940): 13-20.

Ogburn, W.F. "Biography of A.J. Jaffe." In D. Sills (Ed.), International Encyclopedia of the Social Sciences, New York: Macmillan, 1964.

Parsons, Talcott. "Illness and the Role of the Physician: A Sociological Perspective." American Journal of Orthopsychiatry 21, 3 (July, 1951): 452-460.

Riesman, David, Nathan Glazer and Reuel Denney. The Lonely Crowd. New Haven, CT: Yale University Press, 1961.

Robinson, Virginia. A Changing Psychology in Social Casework. Chapel Hill: The University of North Carolina Press, 1930.

Rokeach, Milton. Understanding Human Values. New York: The Free Press, 1979.

Room, Robin. "Ambivalence as a Sociological Explanation: The Case of Cultural Explanations of Alcohol Problems." American Sociological Review 41, 6 (December, 1976): 1047-1065.

Rorabaugh, W.J. The Alcoholic Republic: An American Tradition. New York: Oxford University Press, 1979.

Rush, Benjamin. "An Inquiry into the Effects of Ardent Spirits on the Human Mind and Body, 1795." In Yarnell Henderson (Ed.), A New Deal for Liquor: A Plea for Dilution, Garden City: Doubleday, 1934.

Seward, Jack. The Japanese. New York: Wm. Morrow, 1972.

Slater, P. The Pursuit of Loneliness. Boston: Beacon, 1970.

Sorokin, Pitirim. The Crisis of our Age. New York: Dutton, 1941.

The Statistical History of the United States. Fairfield Publishers, Series D72-122.

Stegh, Leslie Joseph. "Wet and Dry Battles in the Cradle State of Prohibition: Robert J. Bulkley and the Repeal of Prohibition in Ohio." Dissertation, Kent State University, 1975.

Stinchcombe, Arthur. "Social Structure and Organizations." In J.G. March, (Ed.), Handbook of Organizations. Chicago: Rand McNally, 1965.

Stroupe, Henry S. "Social Control by North Carolina Baptist Churches, 1772-1908." North Carolina History Review 52, 2 (1975): 156-170.

Tax, Sal and Larry S. Krucoff. "Social Darwinism." In D. Sills (Ed.), The International Encyclopedia of the Social Sciences, Volume 14, New York: Macmillan, 1968.

Thorner, I. "Ascetic Protestantism and Alcoholism." Psychiatry 16 (1953): 167-175.

Tropman, Elmer J. and J.E. Tropman. "Voluntary Agencies." Forthcoming in Encyclopedia of Social Work, no date.

Tropman, John. "Societal Values and Social Policy." In John Tropman, et al. (Eds.), Strategic Perspectives on Social Policy, Elmsford, NY: Pergamon, 1976.

Tropman, John E. "The Constant Crisis." California Sociologist 1, 1 (1974): 61-87.

Tropman, John and John Erlich. "Introduction to Planning." In F. Cox, et al. (Eds.), Strategies of Community Organization, Itasca, IL: F.E. Peacock, 1979.

Tropman, John and John L. Erlich. "Strategies: An Introduction." In F. Cox, et al. (Eds.), Strategies of Community Organization, 3rd Edition, Itasca: F.E. Peacock, 1979.

Tropman, John E. and Alan Gordon. "The Welfare Threat." Social Forces 57, 2 (December 1978): 697-712.

Turner, James R. "The American Prohibition Movement, 1865-1897." Dissertation, University of Wisconsin, 1972.

Walster, Elaine, H. William Walster and Ellen Berscheid. Equity. Boston: Allyn and Bacon, 1978.

Walton, H., Jr. "Another Force for Disfranchisement: Blacks and the Prohibitionists in Tennessee." Journal of Human Relations 18, 1 (1970): 728-738.

Weber, Max. The Protestant Ethic and the Spirit

of Capitalism. Translated by Talcott Parsons. New York: Scribners, 1956.

Welter, Rush. The Mind of America, 1820-1860. New York: Columbia University Press, 1975.

Williams, Robin. American Society, 3rd Edition. New York: Alfred Knopf, 1970.

Williams, Robin. "Individual and Group Values." In B. Groos (Ed.), Social Intelligence for America's Future, Boston: Allyn and Bacon, 1969.

Williams, Robin. "The Concept of Values." In D.L. Sills (Ed.), International Encyclopedia of the Social Sciences, New York: Macmillan, 1968.

Winkler, Allan M. "Drinking on the American Frontier." Quarterly Journal of Studies on Alcohol 29, 2 (June, 1968): 413-445.

Winkler, Allan M. "Lyman Beecher and the Temperance Crusade." Quarterly Journal of Studies on Alcohol 33, 4 (December, 1972): 939-957.

Woronoff, Jon. Japan: The Coming Social Crisis. Tokyo: Lotus, 1980.

Wortman, C. "Causal Attributions and Personal Control." In Harvey, John H., William J. Ickes, and Robert F. Kidd (Eds.), New Directions in Attrubition Research, Vol. I, Hillsdale, NY: L. Erlbaum Associates (distributed by Wiley and Sons), 1976.

Yinger, Milton. Counter Cultures. New York: Free Press, 1982.

BIBLIOGRAPHY

Allmendinger, David F., Jr. "The Dangers of Ante-Bellum Student Life." Journal of Social History 7, 1 (Fall 1975): 75-85.

Atkinson, J. An Introduction to Motivation. Princeton, NJ: Van Nostrand, 1964.

Bacon, Margaret K. "The Dependency-Conflict Hypothesis and the Frequency of Drunkenness: Further Evidence From a Cross-Cultural Study." Quarterly Journal of Studies on Alcohol 35, 3 (September 1974): 863-876.

Bacon, Selden D. (Special Editor). "Studies of Driving and Drinking." Quarterly Journal of Studies on

Alcohol 28 (May 1968), Supplement No. 4: 1-270.

Bacon, Selden D. "The Classic Temperance Movement of the U.S.A.: Impact Today on Attitudes, Action and Research." British Journal of Addiction 62, 1 (March 1967): 5-18.

Baird, Edward G. "The Alcohol Problem and the Law, Part III: The Beginnings of the Alcoholic-Beverage Control Laws in America." Quarterly Journal of Studies on Alcohol 6, 4 (December 1945): 335-383.

Bales, Robert F. "Cultural Differences in Rates of Alcoholism." Quarterly Journal of Studies on Alcohol 6, 4 (March 1946): 480-499.

Benson, Ronald Morris. "American Workers and Temperance Reform, 1866-1933." Dissertation, University of Notre Dame, 1974.

Bloch, Herbert A. "Alcohol and American Recreational Life." American Scholar 18, 1 (Winter 1948-49): 54-66.

Browing, G.W. "Alcoholism." New York State Journal of Medicine 75 (November 1975): 2324-2325.

Cahalan, Don. Problem Drinkers. San Francisco: Jossey Bass, 1970.

Cahalan, Don, and Robin Room. Problem Drinking Among American Men. New Brunswick, NJ: Publications Division, Rutgers Center of Alcohol Studies (distributed by College and University Press, New Haven, CT), 1974.

Cassedy, J.J. "An Early American Hangover: The Medical Profession and Intemperance, 1800-1860." Bulletin of the History of Medicine 50, 3, (Fall 1976): 405-413.

Cherrington, Ernest H., (Ed.). Standard Encylopedia of the Alcohol Problem. Vol. VI, Westerville, OH: American Issue Publishing Co., 1930.

Cisin, Ira. H. and D. Cahalan. "Comparison of Abstainers and Heavy Drinkers in a National Survey." Psychiatric Research Reports 24 (1968): 10-21.

Cox, Fred M., et al. (Eds.). Strategies of Community Organization. 3rd Edition. Itasca, IL: F.E. Peacock, 1979.

Csikszentmihalyi, M. "A Cross-Cultural Comparison of Some Structural Characteristics of Group Drinking." Human Development 11, 3, (1969): 201-216.

Dawley, Alan and Paul Faler. "Working-Class

Culture and Politics in the Industrial Revolution: Sources of Loyalism and Rebellion." Journal of Social History 9, 4 (Summer 1976): 466-480.

Dorchester, Daniel. The Liquor Problem in All Ages. New York: Phillips and Hunt, 1884.

Dunford, Edward Bradstreet. "The History of the Temperance Movement." Lecture delivered at the Yale School of Alcohol Studies, New Haven, CT, August 2, 1943. Washington, DC: Tem-Press, 1943.

Fairbanks, James D. "Politics, Economics and the Public Morality: State Regulation of Gambling, Liquor, Divorce and Birth Control." Dissertation, Ohio State University, 1975.

Ferneau, E. and R. Gertler. "Attitudes Regarding Alcoholism: Effect of the First Year of the Psychiatry Residency." British Journal of Addiction 66, 4 (December 1971): 257-260.

Filstead, William J., Jean J. Rossi, and Mark Keller, (Eds.). Alcohol and Alcohol Problems: New Thinking and New Directions. Cambridge: Ballinger Publishing Company, 1976.

Furnas, Joseph C. The Life and Times of the Late Demon Rum. New York: Putnam, 1965.

Glatt, M.M. "The English Drinking Problem: Its Rise and Decline Through the Ages." British Journal of Addiction 55 (1959):51-65.

Heath, Dwight B. "Anthropological Perspectives on the Social Biology of Alcohol: An Introduction to the Literature." In Benjamin Kusin and Henri Begleiter (Eds.), Social Aspects of Alcoholism, New York: Plenum Press, 1976.

Kaplan, Paul and I. Hall-McConguodale. "Mother Blaming in Major Clinical Journals." American Journal of Orthopsychiatry 55, 3 (July 1985).

Keller, Mark. "Problems with Alcohol: An Historical Perspective." Chapter 1 in William Filstead, Jean J. Rossi, and Mark Keller, Alcohol and Alcohol Problems. Cambridge, MA: Ballinger Publishing Company, 1976.

Keller, Mark and Vera Efroni. "The Prevalence of Alcoholism." Quarterly Journal of Studies on Alcohol 16, 4 (December 1955): 619-644.

Keller, Mark and Vera Efroni. "The Rate of Alcoholism in the U.S.A., 1954-1956." Quarterly

Journal of Studies on Alcohol 19, 2 (June 1958): 316-319.

Keller, Mark and Vera Efroni. "What Are the Problems Around Alcohol?" StateWays 4 (1974): 25-26.

Knox, Wilma. "Attitudes of Social Workers and Other Professional Groups Toward Alcoholism." Quarterly Journal of Studies on Alcohol 34, 4, Part A (December 1973): 1270-1278.

Kobler, John. Ardent Spirits: The Rise and Fall of Prohibition. New York: Putnam, 1973.

Koren, John. Alcohol and Society. New York: H. Holt and Co., 1916.

Lane, Roger. "Crime and the Industrial Revolution: British and American Views." Journal of Social History 7, 3 (Spring 1974): 287-303.

Linsky, Arnold S. "The Changing Public Views of Alcoholism." Quarterly Journal of Studies on Alcohol 31, 3 (September, 1970): 692-704.

MacKenzie, Frederick Arthur. Sober by Act of Parliament. London: S. Sonnenschein and Sons, Co., Ltd., and New York: Scribner's Sons, 1896.

McCarthy, R.G. "Alcoholism: Attitudes and Attacks, 1775-1935." The Annals of the Academy of Political and Social Science 315 (January 1958): 12-21.

McClelland, D. The Achieving Society. Princeton, NJ: Van Nostrand, 1961.

Mennell, S.J. "Prohibition: A Sociological View." Journal of American Studies 3, 2, (1969): 159-175.

O'Connor, Joyce. "Social and Cultural Factors Influencing Drinking Behavior." Irish Journal Medical Science Supplement. A symposium held in the Royal College of Ireland, October 1974 (June 1975).

Patrick, Clarence H. Alcohol, Culture, and Society. Durham, NC: Duke University Press, 1952.

Phillipson, Richard. "Addiction in the American Armed Forces." The Journal of Alcoholism 5, 4, (Winter 1970): 142-147.

Ray, H.E. "Crime and Prohibition." Journal of Criminal Law and Criminology 38, 2 (July-August 1947): 119-127.

Ray, Oakley S. Drugs, Society, and Human Behavior. St. Louis: The C.V. Mosby Co., 1972.

Rosenbloom, Morris Victor. The Liquor Industry: A Survey of its History, Manufacture, Problems of

Control and Importance. Braddock, PA: Ruffsdale Distilling Co., 1935.

Rotter, Julian B. "Generalized Expectancies for Internal Versus External Control of Reinforcement." Psychological Monographs 80, 1 (1966).

Rowntree, Joseph and Arthur Sherwell. State Prohibition and Local Option. London: Hodden and Stoughton, 1900.

Rubington, Earl. "The Nature of Social Problems." British Journal of Addiction 64, 1 (May 1969): 31-46.

Rubington, Earl and Martin S. Weinberg (Comp.). Deviance: The Interactionist Perspective. New York: MacMillan, 1968.

Rubington, Earl and Martin S. Weinberg (Comp.). The Solution of Social Problems. New York: Oxford University Press, 1973.

Rubington, Earl and Martin S. Weinberg (Comp.). The Study of Social Problems. New York: Oxford University Press, 1971.

Rumbarger, John J. "The Social Origins and Function of the Political Temperance Movement in the Reconstruction of American Society, 1895-1917." Dissertation, University of Pennsylvania, 1968.

Scarr, Sandra. "What's a Parent To Do?" Psychology Today 18, 4 (May 1984).

Siassi, Iradj, Guido Crochetti and Herzl R. Spiro. "Drinking Patterns and Alcoholism in a Blue-Collar Population." Quarterly Journal of Studies on Alcohol 34, 3 (September 1973): 917-926.

Smith, J.A. "Alcohol and Society." Journal of the American Medical Association 217 (6), August 9, 1971, p. 827.

Snyder, Charles R. Alcohol and the Jews. Glencoe, IL: The Free Press, 1958.

Stein, Gary C. "A Fearful Drunkenness: The Liquor Trade to the Western Indians As Seen by European Travelers in America, 1800-1860." Red River Valley History Review 1, 2 (1974): 109-121.

Straus, Robert and Seldon Bacon. Drinking in College. New Haven, CT: Yale University Press, 1953.

Vanderpool, James A. "Self-concept Differences in the Alcoholic Under Varying Conditions of Drinking and Sobriety." Dissertation, Loyola University of Chicago, 1967.

Whyte, William H. The Organization Man. New York: Simon and Schuster, 1956.

Wilson, John and Kenneth Manton. "Localism and Temperance." Sociology and Social Research 59, 2 (January, 1975): 121-135.

Wolfenstein, Martha. "The Emergence of Fun Morality." In Eric Larabee and Rolf Meyersohn (Eds.), Mass Leisure, Glencoe, IL: The Free Press, 1958.

AUTHOR INDEX

Agee, James. 38
Alves, W. and Peter Rossi. 56
Anderson, C. Arnold. 1
Atkinson, J. 69-71
Bacon, Selden D. 31, 48
Banfield, Edward C. and James Q. Wilson. 47
Bell, Daniel. 12, 22
Benedict, Ruth. 9
Billington, Ray H. 19
Brenner, M. Harvey. 66
Cahalan, Don and Ira H. Cisin. 39, 41
Caplan, P. and I. Hale-McCorquodale. 51
City/County Databook. 35
Cohen, Wilbur. ix
Cumming, Elaine. 3
Durkheim, Emile. 52
Edelman, Murray. 3, 4
Erickson, Kai. 4
Fischer, D.H. 28
Gilligan, Carol. 68, 75, 82
Globetti, G. 30
Gouldner. 13
Greer, Germaine. 41, 51
Gronbjerg, Kirsten A. 64
Gusfield, Joseph R. 9, 12, 13, 20, 25, 26, 30, 38, 57, 70
Hawley, Amos H. 52
Hilsman, R. 81
Hirschman, Albert O. 6, 85.
Janowitz, Morris. 9, 27
Jellinek, E.M. 21
Karpfl, Jorn E. and Ernest Vargas. 62
Kates, Don B. 48
Kolb, William L. 2
Krock, Arthur. 29, 32, 36, 48
Lender, Mark. 27
Lifton, Robert J., Shuichi Kato and Michael R. Reich. 15

Linsky, Arnold. 30
Lippmann, Walter. 67
Lipset, Seymour M. ix, 3, 5, 6, 64
Lynd, Robert. 3
Mandler, George. 71
McClelland, D. 67
Meinke, P. 73
Merton, R. 60, 68
Myerson, Abraham. 13
Ogburn, W.F. 2
Parsons, Talcott. 83
Riesman, David, Nathan Glazer and Reuel Denney. 60
Robinson, Virginia. 37
Rokeach, Milton. 3
Room, Robin. 19, 44, 75
Rorabaugh, W.J. ix, 28, 31, 45, 67-72, 75, 78-80, 84
Rush, Benjamin. 33
Seward, Jack. 67
Slater, P. 36
Sorokin, Pitirim. 13
Statistical History of the United States. 35
Stegh, Leslie Joseph. 13
Stinchcombe, Arthur. 17
Stroupe, Henry S. 30
Tax, Sal and Larry S. Krucoff. 62
Thorner, I. 15, 30
Tropman, Elmer J. and J.E. Tropman. 83
Tropman, John E. ix, 3, 55, 56, 62, 64, 83
Tropman, John and John Erlich. xi, 62
Tropman, John E. and Alan Gordon. 64
Turner, James R. 30
Walster, Elaine, H.W. Walster and Ellen Berscheid. 56, 57
Walton, H., Jr. 50
Weber, Max. 2, 16, 21, 79
Welter, Rush. 13, 48
Williams, Robin. 3
Winkler, Allan M. 16, 28
Woronoff, Jon. 11
Wortman, C. 56, 57
Yinger, Milton. 3

SUBJECT INDEX

Abstinence. 20, 48
Alcohol abuse. 20, 35, 43, 47, 74
Alcohol attitudes conflicts. 44
Alcoholics Anonymous. 45
Ambivalence. 4, 18, 19, 30, 37, 39, 40, 59
Antabuse. 34, 45
Anxiety. 18, 67-72, 74, 79, 82-84
Attitudes. 1-7, 12, 14, 15, 23, 26, 27, 30, 39, 40, 42-44, 46, 48, 49, 55, 57, 58, 83
Attitudes toward the poor. 55
Attribution. 55-58
Beer. 11, 29, 37, 47, 63, 68-70, 76
Born-again. 33, 61
Catholic. 16, 17, 19, 20, 31, 57, 61
Cider. 29, 70
Civil War. 30, 48
Clarence Darrow. 32
Conception. 3, 41
Conceptual control. 57
Consumption. 28, 29, 31, 32, 38, 45
Control. 5-23, 25-31, 33-41, 43-51, 53-67, 69, 70, 72-85
Criminal. 31, 34
Cyclical. 7, 12, 65
Diagnoses. 35
Disciplined work force. 29, 35, 38
Drug abuse. 41
Drugs. 38, 39, 54, 63, 64
Egalitarianism. 35
Enemy drinker. 25, 28, 30, 33, 34, 37, 61
Enemy drinker period. 34, 37
Enlightened hedonism. 37, 64
Equality. 3, 5, 6, 8, 55, 72
Free will. 16
Freedom. 6, 16, 18, 26, 36, 41, 71, 84
Freud. 34
Gap theories. 59

Great Rebellion. 30
Guilt. 10, 61, 71, 72, 78, 79, 82
Health. 33, 66
History. 5, 7-9, 11, 14, 15, 17-19, 22, 23, 25, 31, 35, 38, 39, 44-46, 57, 58, 64-66, 76, 83, 84
Hobbsian perspective. 10.
Industrialization. 29
Intellectual control. 57
Inter dimensional conflicts. 65
Interdependence. 52, 77
Intoxication. 27, 28
Intra dimensional conflicts. 65
Japanese. 11, 15, 53, 61, 67
Jews. 19, 77
Laws. 1, 7, 43, 50
Legislative action. 64
Liquor. 13, 28, 29, 40, 45, 69, 70, 84
Locus. 11, 21, 26, 43-45, 50, 53, 58, 59, 62, 65
Locus of control. 11, 21, 26, 43, 58, 59, 62, 65
Lone Ranger. 79
M.A.D.D. (Mothers Against Drunk Driving). 37
Marxism. 63
Mechanical solidarity. 52
Media. 35, 38
Medical. 33-35, 37, 38, 64
Medical model. 35, 38
Mobility. 13, 16, 36, 75
Moral order. 1, 2, 10, 19
Non-Jews. 19
Norm. 5, 27, 56
Norms. 1, 2, 5, 8, 19, 28, 36, 40, 41, 43, 51, 74
Organic solidarity. 52
Outcast. 31
Outlaw. 31
Per capita. 31, 45
Per capita consumption. 31
Permission. 5, 7-14, 16, 18, 19, 21-23, 25-28, 34-41, 43-45, 48, 50-55, 58-67, 69-72, 74-78, 83-85
Permission/control conflicts. 7, 44
Personal control. 15, 47, 55, 57, 84
Philanthropy. 83
Poverty. 20, 34
Power. 2, 28-30, 67, 75, 78, 80
Predestination. 16, 21, 63

Private. 6, 41, 46-48
Prohibition. 11, 30, 32, 34, 45, 48-50
Protestantism. 16, 17, 31, 32, 34
Protestants. 17, 57
Psychiatrists. 34
Psychology. 38
Public. 3, 6, 30, 39, 41, 46, 47, 77
Puritan. 27, 33, 61
Repeal. 30, 32, 33, 37
Responsible drinker. 25, 37, 38, 61, 64, 70
Revivals. 33
Sex. 20, 40, 54
Sexual attitudes. 40
Sick. 25, 26, 31, 33, 34, 37, 38, 41, 55, 61, 70
Sick drinker. 25, 33, 37, 41, 61
Slavery. 29
Sobriety. 29
Social control. 5, 9, 11, 14, 17, 21, 27, 28, 36, 40, 48, 82
Social Darwinism. 62
Social order. 1, 2, 19
Social Security. 37
Speakeasies. 11
Substance abuse. 47, 63
Success. 16, 18, 21, 28, 35, 48, 54, 63, 68, 69, 79
Suffrage. 35
Temperance. 13, 20, 35, 45, 48, 57
Tensions. 32, 83
Tertiary controls. 64
Image of the alcoholic. 55
Values. 1-8, 12, 21, 27, 36, 39-41, 55, 71, 83-85
Victim. 49
Violence. 29, 48-50, 80
Violent. 32, 50, 73
Volstead Act. 30
Washingtonian Society. 45
Whiskey Rebellion. 29, 45
William Jennings Bryan. 32
World War II. 34
Weapon. 73, 74, 80
White collar. 35
Wine. 29, 45, 47, 68-70, 76
Yankee. 73

ABOUT THE AUTHOR

John E. Tropman received his BA in Sociology from Oberlin College, his MA in Social Service Administration from the University of Chicago, and his PhD in Sociology and Social Work from the University of Michigan, where he is a Professor of Social Work and a Faculty Associate at the Institute of Gerontology. He has been a Faculty Associate at the Joint Center for Urban Studies of MIT and Harvard University and Fulbright Lecturer on Social Change in Japan.